MEDAL OF HONOR
AIRBORNE™

PRIMA OFFICIAL GAME GUIDE
WRITTEN BY
MICHAEL KNIGHT

S0-BHS-043

[Prod]uct Manager: Todd Manning
[Edit]or: Rebecca Chastain
[Cop]yeditor: Sara Wilson
[Desi]gn and Layout: Calibre Grafix, LLC
[Man]ufacturing: Suzanne Goodwin

Author Bio

[Mich]ael Knight has worked in the computer/video game industry since 1994 and [has b]een an author with Prima Games for ten years, writing over 60 guides during [that ti]me. Michael has used both his degree in Military History and experience as [a hig]h school teacher to formulate and devise effective strategies and tactics for [gam]es such as the Tom Clancy's Rainbow Six and Hitman series. He has also [cove]red several titles in the *Star Wars* universe including *Star Wars Republic [Com]mando*, *Star Wars Episode III: Revenge of the Sith*, *Star Wars Battlefront II*, and *Star Wars: [Empi]re at War*. Michael has also developed scenarios/missions and written game manuals for SSI, [Sier]ra, [S]torm Entertainment, and Novalogic.

[Wh]en he is not busy at work on an upcoming strategy guide, Michael likes to spend time [with h]is wife and four children at their home in Northern California. It was with their help that [Mich]ael used his abilities and experience to write three travel/strategy guides on Disneyland and [South]ern California, in which he developed tips and hints to help vacationing families save time [and m]oney while maximizing their fun.

[W]e want to hear from you! E-mail comments and feedback to mknight@primagames.com.

[ISBN]: 978-0-7615-5450-9
[Librar]y of Congress Catalog Card Number: 2006934401
[Printe]d in the United States of America

08 09 LL 10 9 8 7 6 5 4 3 2 1

Prima Games
A Division of Random House, Inc.
3000 Lava Ridge Court, Suite 100
Roseville, CA 95661
1-800-733-3000
www.primagames.com

CONTENTS

CONTENTS

THE 82ND AIRBORNE DIVISION

The roots of the American paratrooper go back to the final days of World War I. When the Meuse-Argonne offensive was stalled in October 1918, Billy Mitchell, a major proponent of aviation, approached General Pershing, the commander of the American Expeditionary Force. Mitchell proposed that soldiers from the 1st Infantry Division be loaded onto light bombers and dropped by parachute behind enemy lines. Unfortunately, the stalemate was broken before the idea could be implemented and the war was over the following month.

NOTE

The 82nd Infantry Division was originally formed in 1917 during World War I. Since its members came from all 48 states, the unit was nicknamed the "All Americans."

During U.S. Army training maneuvers in the latter half of the 1930s, some young officers began to consider using airborne troops to secure vital objectives behind enemy lines as a prelude to a larger ground offensive. However, it was not until the spring of 1940 that the U.S. Army got serious about paratroopers.

As the opening wave of the blitzkrieg in western Europe, German paratroopers dropped on the Belgian fortresses at Eben Emael and, in a matter of minutes, rendered them useless. They opened the way for German troops to pour across the border. The German Fallschirmjager (paratrooper) had proven airborne units could attack behind enemy lines to catch the enemy unaware. Furthermore, paratroopers could be used for more than raids. The attacks along the border illustrated their usefulness in supporting the actions of ground troops as part of a larger strategy.

Across the Atlantic, several people were studying the German's use of paratroopers with great interest. In the summer of 1940, General George Marshall, chief of staff of the U.S. Army, decided to create a parachute test platoon of 50 soldiers at Fort Benning, Georgia. Their job was to create procedures for paratroopers, including how to safely jump from a plane. After testing different methods and theories, they developed a training program as well as the way paratroopers would be used in combat. By the fall of that year, a parachute infantry battalion was created to further study how larger units of paratroopers would operate in combat situations. One of the challenges was assembling units after a drop so they could then carry out their objectives.

On May 20, 1941, the German paratroopers were once again used. This time their target was the Mediterranean island of Crete. More than 10,000 paratroopers and glider infantry assaulted the British-held island. Although seaborne German troops were supposed to land to help with the invasion, they were turned back by the British Royal Navy. However, the German airborne forces succeeded in capturing the island against an enemy force more than twice as large as their own.

The German paratroopers suffered heavy casualties, resulting in Crete being the last German airborne operation. However, Marshall saw the value of larger units of paratroopers for carrying out big roles during invasions. He had his eye on the 82nd Infantry Division. Activated in March 1942, its command was given to General Matthew Ridgeway in August and redesignated the 82nd Airborne Division. It was so successful in changing over to this new type of unit that many of its men were transferred a few months later to create the 101st Airborne Division.

The 82nd Airborne Division was sent to North Africa in April 1943. Although they did not take part in Operation Torch (the landings in North Africa), they trained and prepared for their first combat jump. On July 9, 1943, the division parachuted into Sicily to help prevent enemy reinforcements from getting to the beaches where other Allied units were landing. Two months later, the 82nd dropped into Salerno, Italy to help secure the beachhead against German counterattacks.

"The All-American" Soldier

(The song of the 82nd Airborne Division)

Words by Sgt. Carl Sigman

We're All American, and proud to be;
For we're the soldiers of liberty.
Some ride the gliders through the enemy,
Others are sky paratroopers.
We're All American, and fight we will
Till all the guns of the foe are still.
Airborne, from the skies of blue
We're coming through—
Make your jumps, Take your bumps—
Let's go.

Chorus

Put on your boots,
Your parachutes—
Get all those gliders ready
To attack today;
For we'll be gone
Into the dawn
To fight 'em all
The 82nd way—Yes
(Repeat chorus)

By November 1943, the 82nd Airborne was pulled back to England to prepare for their role in the Normandy invasion. On the night of June 5–6, 1944, the division, along with the 101st Airborne and British 6th Airborne divisions, landed. They were some of the first men to fight on this historic day. The division was finally pulled back to England after 33 days of action. During that time, the division received no replacements or reinforcements. It suffered more than 5,000 men killed, wounded, or missing. However, it completed every mission and no ground that they captured was ever lost to the enemy.

The 82nd was assigned the middle part of Operation Market Garden between Grave and Nijmegan, jumping into Holland on September 17, 1944. During the Battle of the Bulge in December 1944, the division was rushed to the Ardennes to help stop the German offensive and turn it back. At the end of the war, the 82nd was send to Berlin to take part in the occupation of Germany.

Since that time, the 82nd Airborne Division has continued to be an active unit. Calling Fort Bragg, North Carolina home, the 82nd Airborne is America's fast reaction force, ready to deploy in a moment's notice. The division has seen action in Central America, Vietnam, the Caribbean, and the Middle East. Recently, they have been sent to both Afghanistan and Iraq.

AIRBORNE TRAINING

So you want to volunteer to be a paratrooper. Before you can pin on those silver jump wings and blouse your pants into your boots, you have some things to learn. That is why you are here for training.

THE INTERFACE

The first thing you must know before you go jumping out of a perfectly good airplane and dropping in on people who want to kill you is how to keep track of your current situation as well as your surroundings. To help make this easier, *Medal of Honor Airborne* has provided a very intuitive interface that appears on your screen and provides all the information you need to know.

The Interface

THE COMPASS

The compass is located in your screen's lower left corner. It contains a lot of information that will help you complete your missions. First off, the "N" on the compass indicates the direction of north in relation to you. The top of the compass is the direction you are facing, so if north is at nine o'clock, for example, you are facing due east.

Icons on the compass provide additional information. The white arrow in the center represents you as well as your facing which is always toward the top of the compass. Green dots represent nearby allies. The closer they are to the center of the compass the closer they are to you. These dots also show the location of these soldiers in relation to you. When the dots are above the white arrow, they are in front of you. Under it, they are behind you. Red German crosses represent enemies. Gold stars show the locations of objectives. If the objective is not close enough to appear on the compass, then it is represented by a golden arrow around the edge of the compass showing the direction to that objective.

TIP

Because every mission has multiple elevations, it is important to know if enemies are on the same level as you. If they are, their icons on the compass will appear bright red. If they are above or below you, the icons will be a faded red. The same goes for allies and objectives—faded colors show that these are on a different level than you are on.

THE HEALTH METER

The health meter is below the compass. To the right of the red cross are four blue segments. Your total health is divided among these segments. As you take damage, the segment on the right begins to drain. If it drains completely, then the next segment on the right begins to drain. When all segments are completely drained, you are dead.

After taking damage and losing some health from one of the segments, if you stop taking damage for a period of time (you move into cover or the threat has been eliminated), that partially depleted segment will begin to recover health. However, segments that were completely depleted remain so. The only way to restore these depleted segments is to pick up a health kit. Each health kit restores one segment of health. Health crates, usually found near landings zones, restore all of your health.

The amount of health with which you begin a mission, as well as how long you must stop taking damage before recovering health, depends on which difficulty level you are playing. At easier levels, you begin with more health and regenerate partially depleted segments faster.

WEAPONS INFORMATION

The interface on the screen also provides information about your weapons. Current weapons are shown near the screen's bottom right side. Icons represent the currently selected grenade and weapon. Below the grenade icon is the number of grenades you have remaining of that type. The two numbers below the weapon icon shows how many rounds you have remaining in your magazine as well as how many additional rounds you are carrying for reloading.

As you use your weapons to kill enemies, you receive kill points which are used to earn weapon rewards—these upgrade your weapon. The weapon icons begin as white outlines. However, they begin to fill with blue as you score kill points. When the icon is completely filled, you receive the weapon award as well as an upgrade. For more information on weapon awards and upgrades, see the next chapter, The Armory.

The reticle in the center of the screen consists of four lines that give you an idea of where your weapon is aimed as well as where your round will hit when fired. The closer these lines are together, the more accurate your fire. However, as you move these lines begin to move apart, representing a decrease in accuracy.

LIST OF OBJECTIVES

During a mission, it is a good idea to check periodically to see what you still need to accomplish. When you pause the game, the Objective screen appears. This lists all the objectives that you have been ordered to complete so far. Next to each objective is a gold star. When that objective is completed, the star appears faded. Some objectives require multiple actions. For example, you may have to destroy AA guns at a specific location. To the right of the objective, it lists how many of these targets remain before that objective is fully completed. Be sure to check this screen often to stay on task.

JUMP SCHOOL

Since you will be jumping into every mission, it is important to know how to parachute well. Therefore, before you head off to Sicily for your first mission, a training center has been established in North Africa at Kairouan where you can do three training jumps.

green light indicates you are over the drop zone and the stick begins to jump out of the plane, one paratrooper after another. Move forward and then continue to move right out the door to jump.

NOTE

If you stand in the doorway and fail to jump, the jumpmaster or another paratrooper will help out by giving you a push.

BASICS OF PARACHUTING

Jumping out of an airplane is one of the safest things a man can do—as long as he follows proper procedure. You always begin inside a C-47 transport. The jumpmaster stands near the doorway. As your plane approaches your drop zone, the pilot turns on the red light. That is the signal for all the paratroopers in your stick to stand and hook up their static line. The

STEERING THE PARACHUTE

After you jump out the door, your parachute opens automatically. You can then use the movement controls to steer the parachute forward or back as well as sideslip to the right or left. The aiming controls are used to look up and down as well as to rotate or turn you while in the air.

For the first drop, you see a bull's-eye on the ground below. A green smoke grenade is in the center. Green smoke indicates a secure zone, or SZ. Steer your parachute so that you land right in the center of the bull's-eye.

NOTE

You may botch this first landing, but that is okay. A botched landing means you did not stay on your feet and it takes a few seconds to get out of your parachute and ready to fight. During combat, it is important to avoid botching landings—especially when enemies are near or you may be dead before you even get a chance to fire your weapon.

FLARING

Another action you can perform while dropping is the flare. To do this, press the Flare button to pull up on the risers. This action slows down your rate of descent as well as your forward motion. Flaring can be used during a jump to stay up in the air longer allowing you to travel farther across an area before landing. A flare only lasts for a second or two, so you may need to flare multiple times. Just remember that it also slows down your forward movement as well. The main reason to flare is for a softer landing. Just as you are about to hit the ground, move forward and press the Flare button. This results in a flared landing that allows you to stay on your feet and get your chute off much quicker than a botched landing.

For your second training jump, you practice flaring. This time, your SZ is to the right of the bull's-eye. Quickly locate the green smoke and center yourself over it. As you approach the ground, move forward and press the Flare button. If you do it correctly, you will receive a message that you flared the landing.

GREASED LANDING

While flaring results in a soft landing, a greased landing gets you out of your chute as quickly as possible. Essentially, you are landing in a forward run with your parachute behind, so as soon as you release the chute, it flies right off you, leaving you ready to fight almost immediately. To perform a greased landing, you must land on level ground and move forward as you are landing. Do not flare as you approach the ground.

The last training jump is a bit tougher. There are three platforms located around the bull's-eye. Flare right as you jump to slow down your descent, giving you time to look around and locate one of these platforms. Pick one and then move toward it. However, unlike before, drop short of it. Then as you get closer, move forward so you are moving over it as you touch down. If you do it correctly, you will perform a greased landing. Notice how quickly you bring up your weapon.

TIP

You are scored on each of your training jumps, for a maximum of 50 points each. The closer you get to the target, the more points you earn. For the first and third jumps, you want to land right on the smoke grenade. However, for the second jump, you want to flare along the arrow on the SZ, landing right at its tip. If you get near-perfect landings on all jumps, you can earn gold wings. Silver and bronze wings are awarded to those who are not as accurate.

FT. BENNING JUMP SCHOOL

Every single paratrooper, from the lowest private up to generals, had to go through jump school at Ft. Benning in Georgia. These men were all volunteers who had at least gone through basic training or may have been in the Army for a number of years. During the four weeks of jump school, these soldiers and officers learned how to pack their own chutes, ride in an airplane and then jump out of it, control their chute during the drop, land safely, meet up with their fellow paratroopers on the ground, and finally how to complete their mission.

The first week of jump school consisted of physical conditioning. The men ran everywhere and went through the obstacle course on a regular basis. In fact, while waiting for dinner, they could either stand at attention or do the obstacle course. Not only did this get the troops in good condition, it also helped weed out those who could not take the intense training.

The second week focused on the skills and techniques needed to parachute safely. They practiced jumping out of mock doors set up just above the ground and even sliding down wires from 35-foot tall towers to practice their landings.

During the third week, lessons included packing the parachutes; every trooper packed his own. Practice drops were now from 250-foot tall towers. They could practice controlling the parachute and the various steps involved in a jump, from embarking on plane to gathering up the chute upon landing.

The final week was the real thing, with five actual drops from an airplane. The first was from 1,200 feet, the second from 1,000 feet, the next two from 800 feet, and the final jump from 1,000 feet again, but this time at night. Following completion of the night jump, the soldier was a paratrooper and could wear the silver jump wings.

COMBAT BASICS

Now that you know how to get from the airplane to the ground, it is time we discuss what to do once you have landed.

MOVEMENT

WALKING AND SPRINTING

Moving around during a mission is fairly simple. By default, you walk while your body is in a standing, upright stance. You can move forward and back as well as strafe to the right and left. To move faster, press the Sprint button. You can sprint as long as you want. However, you can't fire your weapon while sprinting.

STRAFING

Strafing is essentially sidestepping. This is useful when you want to move to one side, but still face the same direction. Strafing is a good way to avoid enemy fire or a grenade while still shooting at a target.

Jumping

Jumping is useful for quickly getting over low obstacles or across gaps. When jumping across a distance, it is best to sprint toward the edge and then jump. This allows you to jump farther than a walking jump.

Crouching

Standing makes you a big target. While enemies are around, it is better to crouch down. Although you move slower in a crouch, you are harder for the enemy to hit and can also hide behind crates and low walls for protection. Pressing the Crouch button toggles you between standing and crouching. While crouched, you can still move and strafe normally.

Crouching when moving up stairs allows you to reach a higher level before your head appears. This enables you to take out enemies more proficiently.

Crouching when moving down stairs also has benefits, as you gain the same advantage: You don't expose yourself until you are almost at the bottom of the steps. Lob a grenade over a stairwell without being seen to take out enemies that normally could pose a serious threat of ambush.

Unless you are certain you have cleared an area, it is best to stay crouched at all times.

Crouch Sprint

During a firefight, you may want to move quickly from one piece of cover to another. That is when the crouch sprint comes in handy. Rather than standing, stay crouched and press the Sprint button as you move. You automatically stand and sprint. Release the Sprint button at your destination to drop down automatically back into a crouch. This saves the time of pressing the Crouch button twice, and may help keep you from getting hit by enemy fire.

Cover

Cover is any object that protects you from enemy fire. It can be a wall, a crate, a vehicle, or even a building. The missions are filled with cover and using it keeps you alive. The enemy uses it and so should you. If you crouch, you can use low objects for cover, then strafe or stand to fire at enemies on the other side.

Combat

Shooting

Shooting is easy. Just press the Fire button or pull the Fire trigger. However, shooting accurately and effectively is another story. Moving greatly reduces your accuracy. Therefore, stay still and crouched while firing. Be sure to take careful aim at your target. This is especially important when using a bolt-action rifle because there is a wait between shots while you chamber the next round. Even though it may take extra time to aim, in the end, doing so saves you time and health if you miss and have to take another shot. Even when using semiautomatic rifles, be sure to correct your aim after every shot.

When firing automatic weapons such as submachine guns, machine guns, and automatic rifles, shoot in short bursts. The recoil on these weapons makes the barrel rise. After shooting a few rounds, you are no longer on target. While spraying an area with automatic fire may seem like a good thing to do, chances are you won't get many hits—if any.

IRONSIGHTS

For even more accuracy, use ironsights. This changes your view so you are looking right over the sights of your weapon with a bit of a zoom. The reticle disappears and you use the actual weapon sight to aim. Hold down the Ironsights button to access this view. When in ironsights, your rounds almost always go right where you are aiming.

PEEKING AND LEANING

While in ironsights, you do not move normally. Instead, your feet are fixed. Strafing to the right or left causes you to lean in that direction. If you are crouched, moving forward causes you to peek up over a low piece of cover. Use peeking and leaning while behind cover. This allows you to fire around or over cover while exposing only a small part of your body.

If you want to actually move while in ironsights view, hold down the Sprint button. Then you can move forward and back as well as strafe rather than peeking and leaning.

Moving while crouched in ironsights is the most accurate way to fire while in motion. It is slow, but it is a good strategy when advancing on an enemy position. Aim at where you expect enemies to appear as you move forward. Then you are ready to fire as soon as they reveal themselves.

SNIPER RIFLES

If you are using a sniper rifle, your ironsights view is through a scope with a crosshairs of some type. The scopes on sniper rifles have an adjustable zoom. At wide zoom, you can see a larger area. This is best for locating a target. Once you have a target, increase your zoom for improved aiming.

To increase your accuracy and prevent the up and down rocking of your crosshairs, control your breathing. If you are playing on the PC, hold down the Hold Breath button. However, if you are playing on the Xbox 360, squeeze the firing trigger slowly. You will see two semicircles along the left side of your scope view move toward the center. When they come together and turn red, you have stopped all the up and down motion of the crosshairs and have the most accurate shot possible. Squeeze the trigger just a bit more to fire. This can be tough and takes some practice, but it is worth it for getting headshots, which kill almost all enemies with a single round.

RELOADING

Keep your weapon fully loaded whenever possible. Running out of ammo in the middle of a firefight can be deadly for you. Therefore, after each quick engagement, reload so you have a full magazine for the next engagement. This is especially true for weapons that are slow to reload.

The M1 Garand is the only weapon you can't top off with a new clip. Instead, you must fire the complete clip before you can load a new one. When using a Garand, just keep track of how many rounds you have loaded at all times, or be ready to switch to a different weapon if you run out.

CHANGING WEAPONS

HOLD ⊙ TO SWAP THOMPSON FOR MP40

As a paratrooper, you always carry a primary weapon, a secondary weapon, and a pistol. You can cycle between these three weapons by pressing the Weapon Cycle button. Quickly select the correct weapon for the task at hand.

During the course of a mission, you can also pick up weapons dropped by enemies or allies as well as weapons that might be at caches or SZs. First select the weapon you want to swap, then press the Action button to complete the trade.

MELEE ATTACKS

If you run out of ammo, or the enem... is too close to shoo... hit the enemy with your weapon. To do this, press the Melee button. It takes several hits to kill an enemy this... way, so keep hitting... until he goes down. Of course, the enemy is probably hittin... you back. Some weapons can be upgraded with a bayonet... dagger, such as the shotgun or MP40. These kill an enemy... with a single hit.

You can kill an enemy with a single blow if you sprint at him and then hit him with a melee attack. In fact, the enemy often goes flying.

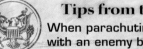

Tips from the Developer

When parachuting into a mission, try lining up with an enemy below—such as one manning a machine gun. Just as you are about to land on top of the enemy, press the Melee button to deliver a deadly blow with your boot, killing the enemy instantly.

GRENADES

Grenades are powerful when used correctly. Grenades cause damage to everyone in their blast radius. However, cover can protect the person from the blast if the cover stands between the detonating grenade and the person. All grenades have a five-second fuse. As soon as you press the Fire button to throw the grenade, you activate the fuse... Hold down the Fire button to "cook off" the grenade. This lets the fuse count down. The main reason to cook grenade... is because the enemy runs away when a grenade lands at their feet. Therefore, try to time it so the grenade explodes before the enemy can react and escape. This takes some practice, but makes grenades very effective.

NOTE

While you can count down yourself as you are cooking a grenade, the ticking sound gets faster as the grenade gets closer to detonation.

Throwing a grenade is an art in itself. You can adjust the angle you throw it at by looking up and down. Grenades can also be thrown to bounce off walls to go around corners or get to places where the enemy is hiding outside of your view. With some practice, you can throw grenades through windows and around cover to hit the enemy where least expected.

When playing on the Xbox 360, you can adjust the power of your throw with the trigger. Pulling the trigger all the way and then releasing throws the grenade with full power. However, just barely pulling the trigger before releasing merely drops the grenade at your feet. The reticle changes in size to represent throwing strength. The larger the reticule, the farther your throw.

TIP

If you time the grenade just right, you can get it to explode in midair right above your target.

THE ARMORY

In *Medal of Honor Airborne*, you are a paratrooper. Every job requires certain types of tools and equipment. Weapons are the tools of a paratrooper. When you begin the campaign, you are assigned a standard loadout of equipment—a Thompson submachine gun, an M1 Garand rifle, a Colt .45 pistol, and four frag grenades. It is important to know how best to use each of these weapons as well as when to use them. During the course of the various missions, you will be able to pick up different weapons. Some are dropped with you while others you must acquire from fallen enemies. Therefore, it is important to study each of the weapons you will encounter.

Marksman Award

Sharpshooter Award

Expert Award

 ## WEAPON AWARDS

As you fight against your enemies, you can earn weapon awards. The icon of your weapon in the lower right corner of the screen fills as you kill enemies. The amount it fills per kill depends on the amount of death points you earn. You receive death points for killing an enemy, making a headshot, making a melee kill, and for the amounts of kills you make in quick succession (at a rate of one per second). Death points are cumulative. Therefore, if you kill an enemy with a headshot, you receive points for both the kill as well as the headshot. Once your weapon icon is full, you will receive the first award—Marksman. Fill up the icon again to receive Sharpshooter, then a third time to earn the Expert award.

Every weapon can be upgraded. In order to improve your weapons, you must earn weapon awards. When you achieve Marksman, you get the first weapon upgrade. The subsequent upgrades are awarded when you earn Sharpshooter and Expert awards. Upgrades can make your weapon more accurate or give you more ammo. Upgrades also carry over from mission to mission. Therefore, concentrate on using only a few weapons to fully upgrade them and get an advantage over your enemies.

 ## SUBMACHINE GUNS

Submachine guns are essentially smaller machine guns that can be carried around easily in battle. Firing a pistol-caliber round, they lack the stopping power of a rifle. However, they make up for this in rate of fire. Submachine guns fire with an automatic action, meaning that they continue to fire as long as you squeeze the trigger until you run out of ammo in the magazine. This type of weapon is best used at close range, though can also be somewhat effective at medium range. During a mission, you should make sure you always have a submachine gun with you.

WEAPONS STATS

Following are descriptions for the stats included for each weapon.

Action: The method a new round is chambered after each shot.

Accuracy: How likely a weapon will hit the target at which it is aimed. The higher the value, the more likely.

Damage: The amount of damage inflicted on a target—the higher the value, the more damage.

Rate of Fire: Representation of how many rounds a weapon can fire in a set amount of time. The higher the value, the greater the number of rounds.

Recoil: This represents the amount the weapon moves off target after each shot. The higher the number, the more the barrel moves.

Reload Rate: This represents the amount of time it takes to reload the weapon. The higher the number, the faster the weapon is to reload.

Player Speed: This is the percentage of normal speed that a player can move while carrying this weapon. 100 is full speed.

Ammo Capacity: This is the number of rounds the weapon can carry in its magazine.

M1928 THOMPSON

The Tommy Gun, a deadly submachine gun firing 700 rounds per minute, is effective at short range. The .45 ACP round delivers knock-down power, but has a significant recoil that requires control.

History

The Thompson was originally designed as a "trench broom" in response the type of warfare that dominated WWI. Troops could use this small machine gun to latterly "sweep" a trench clear of enemies.

WEAPON STATS

Action	Automatic
Accuracy	40
Damage	45
Rate of Fire	85
Recoil	65
Reload Rate	50
Player Speed	90
Ammo Capacity	30

TIP

To minimize the effect of the recoil on your accuracy, fire submachine guns in short bursts. After a few rounds, your aim will be off so much that you won't be hitting your target anyway—only wasting ammo.

UPGRADES

	Name	Effect	Description
	Front Pistol Grip	Improves Accuracy to 50	Forward hand grip provides more accuracy and stability when firing in full auto.
	Cutts Compensator	Decreases recoil to 50	The compensator attaches to the muzzle and deflects the blast upward, reducing muzzle rise to a minimum.
	50 Round Drum Mag	Increases ammo capacity to 50	A huge cylindrical magazine increases the volume of fire with 50 rounds.

MP40 MASCHINENPISTOLE

This light recoil submachine gun fires 500 rounds per minute and is effective at short range. The 9mm round is accurate and easy to manage during rapid fire—but causes less damage.

History

Germany had begun to develop tactics that called for mobile infantry with plenty of automatic firepower—and the submachine gun was easy for untrained men to learn to use. In 1938, the Oberkommando der Wehrmacht (Wehrmacht High Command, OKW) issued a specification for a submachine gun suited to mobile warfare. The Germans chose an automatic-fire-only design. In a nod to the future, the MP40 eschewed wood in favor of plastic and employed a folding metal butt. It retained the blow-back mechanism and telescopic bolt assembly.

WEAPON STATS

Action	Automatic
Accuracy	55
Damage	40
Rate of Fire	55
Recoil	45
Reload Rate	40
Player Speed	95
Ammo Capacity	32

UPGRADES

	Name	Effect	Description
	Dual Magazines	Increases reload rate to 70	Two magazines taped together allow a quick reload with a fresh 32 mag at the ready.
	64 Round Magazine	Increases ammo capacity to 64	A prototype magazine assembly for the MP40-II. Two magazines welded together give a huge 64 round capacity.
	SS Dagger	Increases melee damage	A close-combat melee weapon that can kill in one strike.

RIFLES

Rifles are the main weapon of the infantry. Firing a larger round through a longer barrel, a rifle has a longer range, greater accuracy, and more stopping power than a submachine gun. It takes only two hits to the body, or one to the head, to bring down an enemy when firing a rifle. Since their rate of fire is less than a submachine gun, rifles are best used at medium to long range where you have the time to take careful aim before shooting. Rifles fire only one round at a time. It is a good idea to keep a rifle with you for engaging enemies at a distance.

M1 GARAND

An accurate and effective battle rifle, the M1 can deliver damage very accurately and quickly at long range. It is semiautomatic, but has a small ammo capacity.

History

During WWII, more than 4 million M1 rifles were produced. Their semi-automatic rate of fire allowed a U.S. soldier to put out a lot more firepower than an enemy with a bolt-action rifle.

NOTE

The M1 Garand uses an eight-round stripper clip to load its ammunition. While this makes it quick to reload, it also prevents you from reloading in the middle of a clip. Instead, you must fire off all eight rounds before you can load another clip.

WEAPON STATS

Action	Semi Auto
Accuracy	85
Damage	85
Rate of Fire	35
Recoil	50
Reload Rate	50
Player Speed	88
Ammo Capacity	8

UPGRADES

	Name	Effect	Description
	Match Grade Barrel	Increases accuracy to 90	A precision-made barrel that increases accuracy in all aspects.
	Lock Bar Adjustable Sights	Increases accuracy to 95, increases zoom	A variable sight that allows a range of adjustment.
	M7A1 Grenade Launcher	Adds grenade launch capability	A barrel attachment that allows firing of a MKII Frag grenade from the muzzle.

K98K KARABINER KURTZ

This bolt-action rifle can take out a target with one well-placed shot. Effective at long range, it has a slow rate of fire and slow reloads.

History

An enormous number of extras were developed to enable additional capabilities including a grenade launching device, folding butts, and periscopes. Weapons that tested to be extremely accurate from the factory were equipped with scopes and used as sniper rifles. The K98 remained in production until the end of the war.

WEAPON STATS

Action	Bolt Action
Accuracy	90
Damage	100
Rate of Fire	15
Recoil	70
Reload Rate	20
Player Speed	87
Ammo Capacity	5

UPGRADES

	Name	Effect	Description
	Polished Match Grade Bolt	Increases rate of fire to 25	A precision-made bolt assembly that allows increased rate of fire with faster lock up time.
	5 Round Stripper Clip	Increases reload rate to 45	An assembled clip of 5 rounds that can be quickly inserted for a fast full reload.
	Schiessbecher Grenade Launcher	Adds grenade launch capability	A barrel attachment that fires a 30mm grenade from the muzzle. The 30mm is more powerful than the MKII Frag.

AUTOMATIC RIFLES

As a result of the machine gun's domination of the battlefield during WWI as a defensive weapon, various armies sought to create a machine gun that could be carried during an advance. The desire for "portable" machine guns led to the development of automatic rifles. Their purpose was to lay down suppressing fire so that infantry armed with rifles and submachine guns could then flank the enemy while they kept their heads down. However, these weapons could also be used on their own to engage the enemy. Less accurate than a rifle, but with the same stopping power and a high rate of fire, automatic rifles are best used at medium range and fired in short bursts.

M1918 BROWNING AUTOMATIC RIFLE (BAR)

The BAR is an automatic rifle that delivers very heavy damage at a controllable 450 rounds per minute. Effective at medium range, it can be very accurate in bursts, but heavy recoil can diminish accuracy with sustained fire.

History

According to U.S. Army tactics during WWII, each infantry squad was to have one BAR, which was referred to as the "squad's base of fire." However, if a squad could, they would try to get an additional BAR for increased firepower.

WEAPON STATS

Action	Automatic
Accuracy	70
Damage	85
Rate of Fire	55
Recoil	80
Reload Rate	40
Player Speed	85
Ammo Capacity	20

UPGRADES

	Name	Effect	Description
	Compensator	Decreases recoil to 70	A compensator that deflects muzzle blast significantly, reducing recoil and muzzle rise during full auto fire.
	A2 Adjustable Sights	Increases accuracy to 75, increases zoom	A variable sight that allows a range of adjustment.
	Dual Magazines	Increases reload rate to 60	Two magazines attached side by side makes another 20 rounds ready for a quick reload.

StG.44 SturmGewehr

This assault rifle is one of the most devastating weapons in the war. Deadly accurate at 550 rounds per minute and effective at medium range, it's a one-man assault squad.

History

German evaluations of combat in WWI and the beginning of WWII determined infantry engagements were occurring at ranges where they were often decided by the amount of firepower that could be brought to bear. The MP40 proved a success for close- and short-range combat, but was ineffective at intermediate ranges and lacked the killing power of a rifle. A solution was sought by taking the best aspects of a rifle and the best aspects of a submachine gun and combining them into a new type of weapon. Its introduction to the eastern front in 1944 was an unqualified success and these weapons were highly sought after by all combatants.

WEAPON STATS

Action	Automatic
Accuracy	60
Damage	65
Rate of Fire	50
Recoil	75
Reload Rate	40
Player Speed	88
Ammo Capacity	30

UPGRADES

	Name	Effect	Description
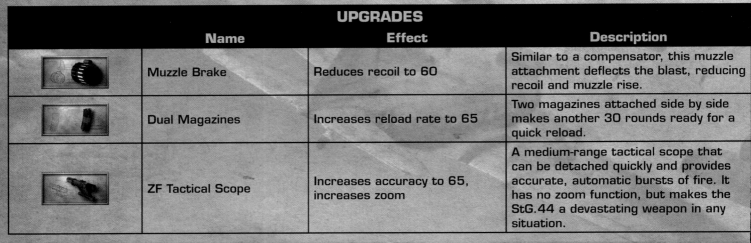	Muzzle Brake	Reduces recoil to 60	Similar to a compensator, this muzzle attachment deflects the blast, reducing recoil and muzzle rise.
	Dual Magazines	Increases reload rate to 65	Two magazines attached side by side makes another 30 rounds ready for a quick reload.
	ZF Tactical Scope	Increases accuracy to 65, increases zoom	A medium-range tactical scope that can be detached quickly and provides accurate, automatic bursts of fire. It has no zoom function, but makes the StG.44 a devastating weapon in any situation.

SNIPER RIFLES

The sniper rifle is designed for engaging enemies at long range. Firing a rifle-caliber, high grain round, these rifles are extremely accurate. They are often equipped with a scope to improve accuracy. Able to kill with a single, well-aimed shot, a sniper at long range can take the time to make each shot count without worrying about return fire.

M1903 SPRINGFIELD SNIPER

A precision instrument, the M1903 is fitted with a scope and can take out most targets with one shot to the head or chest. Effective at long range, it has a slow rate of fire and slow reloads.

History The M1903 rifle was the primary weapon for the U.S. Army during WWI and continued to be used after the introduction of the M1 Garand as weapons for snipers.

WEAPON STATS	
Action	**Bolt Action**
Accuracy	100
Damage	130
Rate of Fire	15
Recoil	65
Reload Rate	20
Player Speed	80
Ammo Capacity	5

TIP

When sniping, it is always a good idea to stay behind cover and then pop up or peek around the cover when you are ready to fire. Also, when focusing on a target at long range through your scope, it is easy for other enemies to approach on your flanks or from behind. Therefore, stay aware of your situation.

UPGRADES

	Name	Effect	Description
	Polished Match Grade Bolt	Increases rate of fire to 25	A precision-made bolt assembly that allows increased rate of fire with faster lock up time.
	5 Round Stripper Clip	Increases reload rate to 45	An assembled clip of 5 rounds that can be quickly inserted for a fast, full reload.
	M1 Grenade Launcher	Adds grenade launch capability	A barrel attachment that allows firing of a MKII Frag grenade from the muzzle.

G43 GEWEHR

Also known as the Kar.43, this rifle is semiautomatic and can be fitted with a scope. It is effective at long range with good ammo capacity.

History

The Germans first begin to design this semiautomatic rifle in 1941 after encounters on the Eastern Front with Russian semiautomatic rifles. All G43s were produced with a scope rail so that a scope could be easily attached to any of these rifles for sniper operations.

WEAPON STATS

Action	Semi Auto
Accuracy	85
Damage	75
Rate of Fire	30
Recoil	55
Reload Rate	50
Player Speed	85
Ammo Capacity	10

Tips from the Developer

You will be amazed at the distances at which you can engage a group of enemies. With a trusty sniper rifle in tow, you can dispatch enemy troops from across the map. The trick is to find a good perch from which to conduct your long-distance hot lead injections.

UPGRADES

Name	Effect	Description
20 Round Magazine	Increases ammo capacity to 20	A prototype magazine with twice the round capacity.
ZF4 Scope	Increases accuracy to 100, adds adjustable zoom	An effective long-range sniper scope that allows greater accuracy. Combined with the G43 semiautomatic it makes a deadly sniper rifle.
Schiessbecher Grenade Launcher	Adds grenade launch ability	A barrel attachment that allows firing of a 30mm grenade from the muzzle. The 30mm is more powerful than the MKII Frag.

PISTOLS

Pistols are considered a secondary weapon, to be used when you are out of ammo for other weapons or need a quick-firing weapon for close-range combat. They are not very accurate and only effective up close. However, if your clip runs out in the middle of a firefight, it is faster to switch to your pistol than reload your submachine gun or rifle.

M1911 COLT .45 PISTOL

The 1911 delivers stopping power with every shot at close range. It has significant recoil and a 7-round magazine.

History During WWII, move European armies issued handguns only to officers as a badge of rank. The U.S. Army, on the other hand, considered handguns a valuable weapon for not only officers, but also for enlisted men who would not have a rifle, such as crew for artillery, drivers, tankers, etc. Though unauthorized, paratroopers and infantry soldiers carried handguns they brought with them or received from home as a weapon of last resort and for peace of mind. If an enemy jumps into your foxhole with you, a pistol is a lot more useful than a much longer rifle.

WEAPON STATS

Action	Semi Auto
Accuracy	35
Damage	50
Rate of Fire	20
Recoil	30
Reload Rate	70
Player Speed	100
Ammo Capacity	7

UPGRADES

	Name	Effect	Description
	Leather Holster	Decreases weapon swap time.	Allows a faster weapon draw time.
	Match Grade Trigger	Increases rate of fire to 35	Allows faster firing with accuracy.
	Magnum Rounds	Increases damage to 100	Special ammo with increased power that drops a target in one hit.

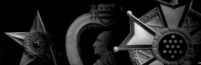

C96 MAUSER

It is known as the "Broom Handle," a very accurate pistol effective at close range. It has a larger 10 round magazine, but the 9mm causes less damage.

History

One of the first semiautomatic pistols to be used in great numbers, the C96 Mauser was first produced in 1896. Unlike most pistols of this type, where the magazine fit into the grip, the C96 placed the magazine in front of the trigger. Some sources state that Winston Churchill, the Prime Minister of Great Britain during WWII, carried a C96 into battle during the Second Boer War.

WEAPON STATS

Action	Semi Auto
Accuracy	40
Damage	30
Rate of Fire	35
Recoil	25
Reload Rate	50
Player Speed	100
Ammo Capacity	10

Tips from the Developer

The Mauser can be found in a safe by the control room in the tank factory in the Varsity Factory mission. Use it so you can earn all three upgrades. You can't beat an automatic weapon that is very accurate with unlimited ammo.
—Robert Heckv

UPGRADES

	Name	Effect	Description
	Shoulder Stock	Decreases recoil to 20	The wooden stock allows shouldering of the weapon, reducing recoil and muzzle climb to a minimum.
	20 Round Magazine	Increases ammo capacity to 20	The box magazine provides twice the round capacity and a faster reload.
	712 Conversion Kit	Increases rate of fire to 100	Schnellfeuer mechanism allows full-automatic fire at 1,000 rounds per minute.

ANTI-TANK

Anti-tank weapons are designed to destroy enemy armored vehicles such as tanks. These fire rocket-propelled rounds that explode on impact. You can also use these weapons against infantry. They cause splash damage to nearby enemies—you don't even have to get a direct hit.

M18 RECOILLESS RIFLE

The M18 fires a high explosive artillery shell at high velocity. It is extremely heavy and very slow to reload.

History

 Firing a 57mm rocket-propelled shell, the M18 was more accurate than the bazooka due to its rifled barrel. In addition, the larger round was more effective against tanks, able to penetrate one inch of armor at ranges of up to two and a half miles.

WEAPON STATS	
Action	**Single Shot**
Accuracy	90
Damage	600
Damage Radius	1,000
Rate of Fire	5
Recoil	50
Reload Rate	20
Player Speed	70
Ammo Capacity	1

UPGRADES			
	Name	**Effect**	**Description**
	Enhanced Scope	Increases accuracy to 95, adds adjustable zoom	A variable sight that allows a range of adjustment.
	Satchel	Increases amount of rockets carried by 3	A bag to store more shells. Allows more shells to be carried.
	Musette Bag	Increases amount of rockets carried by another 3	A larger bag to store more shells. Allows more shells to be carried.

RPzB 54 PANZERSCHRECK

The Tank Terror is a rocket-propelled weapon good at long range. The 88mm rocket is easy to reload and has good armor penetration, but the weapon is very bulky and heavy.

History

The Panzerschreck was similar to the U.S. bazooka in that it had a reusable tube which launched an armor-piercing rocket. The backblast of this weapon could be deadly to the soldier firing it, who had to wear a gas mask and special fireproof poncho for safety. A protective shield was added to make mask and poncho unnecessary.

WEAPON STATS

Action	Single Shot
Accuracy	90
Damage	450
Damage Radius	900
Rate of Fire	10
Recoil	40
Reload Rate	25
Player Speed	75
Ammo Capacity	1

Tips from the Developer

Anti-tank weapons are affected by gravity. If you are firing an anti-tank weapon a great distance, you will need to aim above the target to compensate for the effects of gravity.

UPGRADES

	Name	Effect	Description
x2	Improved Sights	Increases accuracy to 95, increases zoom	A variable sight that allows a range of adjustment.
	Shell Bag	Increases amount of rockets carried by 3	A bag to store more shells. Allows more shells to be carried.
	Shell Bag	Increases amount of rockets carried by another 3	A larger bag to store more shells. Allows more shells to be carried.

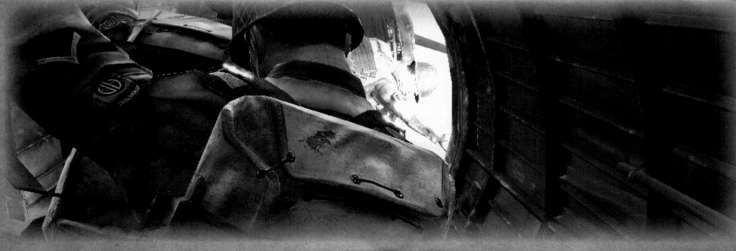

CLOSE COMBAT

Some weapons are designed for fighting up close and personal. The shotgun is a perfect weapon for close-quarters combat. Firing several small projectiles that spread out means you don't have to take time to aim carefully before pulling the trigger. Plus, if you don't kill an enemy as you are rushing toward him, you can always use the shotgun for a melee attack.

M12 SHOTGUN

A powerful and devastating weapon, the 12-gauge is effective against groups of enemies in close quarters. It is slow to reload and has limited range.

History Originally referred to as a trench gun due to its use in WWI, the M12 was produced by Winchester. Unlike a standard 12-gauge shotgun, the M12 featured a handguard and bayonet mount.

WEAPON STATS

Action	Pump Action
Accuracy	20
Damage	75
Rate of Fire	20
Recoil	90
Reload Rate	25
Player Speed	90
Ammo Capacity	8

UPGRADES

	Name	Effect	Description
	Modified Choke	Improves accuracy to 40	A tighter choke on the barrel constricts the shot pattern, allowing greater accuracy at longer ranges.
	Magnum Rounds	Increases damage to 95	Powerful 12-gauge shells deliver heavier damage and more knockdown power.
	M1 16" Bayonet	Increases melee damage	A huge bayonet attached to the lug on the barrel heat shield that delivers devastating one-hit melee kills with a longer reach.

Grenades are considered indirect weapons. That means you do not have to have a line of sight to the target in order to attack. Instead, you can throw a grenade over an object the enemy is using for cover, or—with the exception of Gammon grenades—bounce them off walls and around corners to hit unseen enemies as well. Standard grenades have a five-second fuse. Since the enemy will run away when a grenade lands at their feet, "cook off" a grenade by pulling the pin and holding it for two to three seconds before throwing it so that you time it to explode just as it reaches your target.

No.82 Gammon Grenade

An elastic bag stuffed with a large amount of plastic explosive and armed with an Always Fuze. It has massive damage potential.

History

This was a very interesting grenade that could be stuffed with different amounts of plastic explosive, depending on the target. The Always Fuze would arm in flight and then explode on contact. It got its name because the fuse would detonate no matter which way the grenade landed. The Gammon grenade was effective against armored vehicles such as tanks. In the game, the Gammon grenade has a five-second fuse like the other grenades.

WEAPON STATS

Action	Thrown
Damage	700
Rate of Fire	800
Player Speed	100
Ammo Capacity	1

UPGRADES

	Name	Effect	Description
	Satchel	Increases amount of grenades carried by 3	A bag designed to hold more grenades.
	Bandolier	Increases amount of grenades carried by 3 more	A bag designed to hold more grenades.
	Musette Bag	Increases amount of grenades carried by 3 more	A bag designed to hold more grenades.

MKII Fragmentation Grenade

A metal body stuffed with an explosive charge designed to break up into multiple fragments. The fuse can be shortened by cooking the grenade.

WEAPON STATS

Action	Thrown
Damage	250
Damage Radius	650
Player Speed	100
Ammo Capacity	1

History This grenade's body was cast iron. The serrations that gave the grenade its pineapple appearance were designed to create about 1,000 lethal fragments. While the grenade could be thrown about 100 feet, fragments could be dangerous up to 150 feet. Therefore, troops were trained to duck until their grenade detonated.

UPGRADES

	Name	Effect	Description
	Satchel	Increases amount of grenades carried by 2	A bag designed to hold more grenades.
	Bandolier	Increases amount of grenades carried by 2 more	A bag designed to hold more grenades.
	Musette Bag	Increases amount of grenades carried by 2 more	A bag designed to hold more grenades.

MODEL 24 STIELHANDGRANATE

The Stick grenade, or Potato Masher, is a heavy metal that can be filled with explosive and attached to a wooden handle.

History Though larger than MKII grenade, the Model 24, with its wooden handle acting like a lever, could be thrown almost twice as far.

WEAPON STATS

Action	Thrown
Damage	350
Damage Radius	750
Player Speed	100
Ammo Capacity	1

UPGRADES

	Name	Effect	Description
	Satchel	Increases amount of grenades carried by 2	A bag designed to hold more grenades.
	Bandolier	Increases amount of grenades carried by 2 more	A bag designed to hold more grenades.
	Musette Bag	Increases amount of grenades carried by 2 more	A bag designed to hold more grenades.

THE ENEMY

As important as it is to know your weapon, it is also vital to know your enemy. During the missions, you will face 10 enemies. While all are trained and dangerous, those in the earlier missions are relatively tame compared to those you face in the final couple of missions. Before each mission, look at the opposition you will face. Then you will know what to expect and how best to defeat them.

THE ARTIFICIAL INTELLIGENCE

Medal of Honor Airborne uses a unique system to control the nonplayer characters (NPC) including both the Axis enemies and your allies—the paratroopers who fight alongside you.

Because you can drop into a mission anywhere within your drop zone, then advance on objectives in whichever order you choose, the artificial intelligence (AI) must be able to respond to a great number of possibilities. As a result, the AI-controlled NPCs' actions can't be scripted as they are in many first-person shooter games. Instead, each NPC must think for himself and react according to his surroundings.

To accomplish this, the game developers created a new way of programming the AI. The result is the Affordance Engine. In a nutshell, this engine gives each NPC a series of processes such as selecting targets, moving into cover, detecting and prioritizing threats, and so forth. The information in this chapter will help you understand how individual types of enemies will react differently. For more on the Affordance Engine, see the next chapter on Tactics.

NOTE

Two of the stats listed for each enemy are battle experience and combat effectiveness.

Battle experience refers to how the NPC reacts to his enemies—you and your allies. The more experience he has, the more likely he is to use cover effectively, fire in shorter controlled bursts, and blind fire around cover. In addition, the higher the experience, the more aggressive the soldier. There are six different levels of battle experience.

Combat effectiveness is a measure of how much damage the NPC can inflict as well as the amount of damage he can receive before dying. The higher the combat effectiveness, the greater the damage—even if the NPC is using the same weapon as a less effective NPC. This is due to the way the weapon is used and the accuracy of the firer. There are ten different levels of combat effectiveness.

ITALIAN BLACKSHIRT

PRIMARY WEAPON	K98k Karabiner Kurtz Rifle
SECONDARY WEAPON	Model 24 Stielhandgranate
BATTLE EXPERIENCE	Trained
COMBAT EFFECTIVENESS	1
MISSION APPEARANCES	Husky

The Italian Blackshirt is the standard infantry you face during the first part of Operation Husky as you go after the initial objectives. While they are the weakest of the enemies, they can still cause you damage. Armed with a bolt-action rifle, they only take a shot or two before getting behind cover. While they do move into an area that is under their control or vacated by the Americans, they do not pursue. Rather, they try to reclaim that territory they might have lost. Occasionally a Blackshirt throws a grenade.

Historical Note

"The Blackshirts" was the name given to the supporters of Fascist leader Benito Mussolini during his rise to power—essentially Il Duce's muscle—due to their black uniforms. During the war, the Blackshirts fought alongside the Italian Army in North Africa and other campaigns. However, unlike the army, their loyalty was first to Mussolini.

VICECAPO BLACKSHIRT

PRIMARY WEAPON	MP40 Maschinenpistole Submachine Gun
SECONDARY WEAPON	Model 24 Stielhandgranate
BATTLE EXPERIENCE	Trained
COMBAT EFFECTIVENESS	1
MISSION APPEARANCES	Husky

Armed with a submachine gun, the Vicecapo Blackshirts behave similarly to the regular Blackshirts. They, too, are found only during the initial objectives of Operation Husky as they help defend the AA guns from the paratroopers. Due to their weapon's high rate of fire, the Vicecapo Blackshirts can cause more damage than their fellow Italians.

TROPICAL HEER INFANTRY

PRIMARY WEAPON	MP40 Maschinenpistole Submachine Gun
SECONDARY WEAPON	Model 24 Stielhandgranate
BATTLE EXPERIENCE	Skilled
COMBAT EFFECTIVENESS	2
MISSION APPEARANCES	Husky

The Heer infantry is the standard soldier in the German Army. The tropical variety are found only in Operation Husky during the later part of the mission. Not as experienced as their European counterparts, the Tropical Heer Infantry carry submachine guns and can still cause a lot of damage. They occasionally use grenades to attack enemies behind cover.

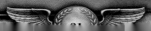

HEER OFFICER

PRIMARY WEAPON	MP40 Maschinenpistole Submachine Gun
SECONDARY WEAPON	Model 24 Stielhandgranate
BATTLE EXPERIENCE	Proven
COMBAT EFFECTIVENESS	3
MISSION APPEARANCES	Husky, Avalanche

While armed the same as the Tropical Heer Infantry, the Heer Officer has more experience and is more effective during combat. These soldiers are also more likely to throw grenades.

EUROPEAN HEER INFANTRY

PRIMARY WEAPON	G43 Gewehr Rifle
SECONDARY WEAPON	Model 24 Stielhandgranate
BATTLE EXPERIENCE	Skilled
COMBAT EFFECTIVENESS	3
MISSION APPEARANCES	Avalanche, Neptune

European Heer Infantry are more effective than their Tropical counterparts and are also armed with rifles. Although the rifles do not have as high a rate of fire as the other Heer troops' weapons, the European Heer Infantry can cause more damage with their weapons due to the rifle's greater accuracy and greater damage inflicted per round.

WAFFEN INFANTRY

PRIMARY WEAPON	MP40 Maschinenpistole Submachine Gun
SECONDARY WEAPON	Model 24 Stielhandgranate
BATTLE EXPERIENCE	Proven
COMBAT EFFECTIVENESS	4
MISSION APPEARANCES	Avalanche, Neptune, Market Garden

The Waffen infantry are the more elite soldiers in Operation Avalanche. However, they are the basic units during both Neptune and Market Garden missions. Due to their use of a submachine gun, Waffen Infantry are deadlier at close range.

Historical Note

The Waffen were a separate organization than the German Heer (Army). The Waffen were actually the military arm of the Schutzstaffel or SS, the security force for the Nazi party. As such, Waffen soldiers' loyalty was to Hitler. Waffen units were usually the elite, receiving better equipment and supplies than the standard army.

WAFFEN OFFICER

PRIMARY WEAPON	StG.44 Sturmgewehr Automatic Rifle
SECONDARY WEAPON	Model 24 Stielhandgranate
BATTLE EXPERIENCE	Veteran
COMBAT EFFECTIVENESS	5
MISSION APPEARANCES	Neptune, Market Garden, Flak Tower

Waffen officers appear during the middle missions and are bigger threats than Waffen Infantry due to their greater experience as well as their more powerful weapons. The automatic rifle they carry can be deadly at close and medium range.

WAFFEN SENIOR TROOPER

PRIMARY WEAPON	G43 Gewehr Rifle
SECONDARY WEAPON	None
BATTLE EXPERIENCE	Veteran
COMBAT EFFECTIVENESS	6
MISSION APPEARANCES	Market Garden, Varsity

Although they are not armed with the sniper version of the G43 rifle, Waffen senior troopers act as the German snipers during Operation Market Garden. They usually are found in elevated positions from which they fire down on the enemy below. They do not throw grenades. However, they tend to pursue or hunt you during a mission if on the same height level.

WAFFEN STORM LEADER

PRIMARY WEAPON	StG.44 Sturmgewehr Automatic Rifle
SECONDARY WEAPON	Model 24 Stielhandgranate
BATTLE EXPERIENCE	Elite
COMBAT EFFECTIVENESS	6
MISSION APPEARANCES	Varsity, Flak Tower

Appearing only in the latter two missions, the Waffen Storm Leader is very aggressive and not afraid to fight. In addition to firing an automatic rifle, they also like to throw grenades. Therefore, when you see one of these enemies, be ready either to move away from a grenade, or to kick it back at the thrower.

FALLSCHIRMJAGER INFANTRY

PRIMARY WEAPON	G43 Gewehr Rifle
SECONDARY WEAPON	Model 24 Stielhandgranate
BATTLE EXPERIENCE	Veteran
COMBAT EFFECTIVENESS	7
MISSION APPEARANCES	Market Garden, Varsity, Flak Tower

Fallschirmjager infantry are the most elite of the standard infantry units and are quite deadly with their semiautomatic rifles. They like to maneuver during a firefight, moving quickly from cover to cover, making it tougher to line up a shot at long range. Watch for their grenades because Fallschirmjager throw them not only to kill enemies behind cover, but to distract enemies while they move into a better position.

Historical Note

The Fallschirmjager were the German paratroopers. Like their American counterparts, they were considered the elite of the German military and actually part of the Luftwaffe, or air force, rather than the army. While they took part in airborne operations during the invasions of Holland and Belgium, as well as the all-airborne invasion of Crete, by the middle to end of the war, they stayed on the ground in the role of elite infantry.

FALLSCHIRMJAGER COMMANDER

PRIMARY WEAPON	StG.44 Sturmgewehr Automatic Rifle
SECONDARY WEAPON	Model 24 Stielhandgranate
BATTLE EXPERIENCE	Veteran
COMBAT EFFECTIVENESS	8
MISSION APPEARANCES	Market Garden, Varsity, Flak Tower

If the Fallschirmjager are the best of the standard infantry units, then the Fallschirmjager commander is even better. They have a higher combat effectiveness and a deadlier weapon, so watch out for these troops during a fight. Be sure to find cover or you will be killed.

FALLSCHIRMJAGER SNIPER

PRIMARY WEAPON	G43 Gewehr Sniper Rifle
SECONDARY WEAPON	None
BATTLE EXPERIENCE	Elite
COMBAT EFFECTIVENESS	8
MISSION APPEARANCES	Varsity, Flak Tower

Fallschirmjager snipers always take up elevated positions, such as on top of buildings or other high structures. Armed with a sniper rifle, they are extremely accurate and can cause a lot of damage with each hit. Since their sniper rifle is semiautomatic, they can fire quite rapidly compared to other snipers. Watch for the sunlight glinting off their scopes since this is a telltale sign of their location. Often you need a sniper rifle of your own to kill these deadly hunters.

PANZERGRENADIER

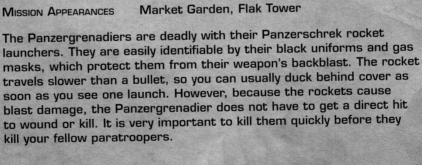

PRIMARY WEAPON	RPzB 54 Panzerschreck
SECONDARY WEAPON	None
BATTLE EXPERIENCE	Special
COMBAT EFFECTIVENESS	9
MISSION APPEARANCES	Market Garden, Flak Tower

The Panzergrenadiers are deadly with their Panzerschrek rocket launchers. They are easily identifiable by their black uniforms and gas masks, which protect them from their weapon's backblast. The rocket travels slower than a bullet, so you can usually duck behind cover as soon as you see one launch. However, because the rockets cause blast damage, the Panzergrenadier does not have to get a direct hit to wound or kill. It is very important to kill them quickly before they kill your fellow paratroopers.

NAZI STORM ELITE

PRIMARY WEAPON	MG42 Maschinengewehr Light Machine Gun
SECONDARY WEAPON	None
BATTLE EXPERIENCE	Special
COMBAT EFFECTIVENESS	10
MISSION APPEARANCES	Varsity, Flak Tower

The Nazi Storm Elite is the ultimate soldier. Armed with the same machine gun you face from mounted positions, this enemy advances toward you while firing long bursts from his weapon. Not only can these soldiers put out a lot of firepower, they also can take a lot of damage. While Nazi Storm Elite soldiers never take cover, they do move away from grenades that land close to them. Therefore, when using Gammon grenades, which are the best for tackling this enemy, be sure to cook them so they detonate shortly after landing near your target. Nazi Storm Elites are also very vulnerable to headshots. A couple of hits with a sniper rifle usually does the trick. However, if they are close, use an automatic rifle and aim at the enemy's chest so that as your weapon recoils and your aim goes up, you catch the Nazi Storm Elite with a few rounds to the head. You face a couple of these during Operation Varsity and lots more during the Flak Tower mission.

AIRBORNE WARFARE TACTICS

Having covered the basics of combat, the specifics of weapons, and the types of enemies against which you must fight, it is time to combine all three into methods for achieving victory—tactics.

JUMPING INTO A MISSION

WHERE TO LAND

The overall drop zone for most missions is quite large. It can be limited to a part of the map or even include the entire map area. Therefore, your choices of places to touch down are many. Before you select a spot to land, you must know what you want to do. If you do not know what you want to do, it really does not matter where you land.

At the start of every mission, you must parachute down to the ground. Because of this, each time you play a mission can be different, depending on where you land. While you have already trained in the skills necessary to steer a parachute and perform a successful landing, another important part of being an airborne trooper is knowing where you want to land.

There are several factors you must consider when determining your landing spot. First, what objective are you going to go for first? That alone helps narrow down the best area within the drop zone. You usually want to land as close to an objective as possible.

Enemy presence is another factor. While you might be able to drop right on the objective, these locations are usually heavily defended and if you drop there, you will be lucky to get out of your parachute before being killed. Therefore, look for a spot where you can land without coming under immediate enemy fire. If it is close to the enemy, then does it at least have cover between you and the enemy?

The final factor is the advantage the landing spot provides. This could be a high elevation that allows you to fire down on the enemy below or a spot that lets you flank or attack the enemy from the rear. By landing in certain areas, you can bypass some of the enemy's defenses.

LANDING SPOT FACTORS

1. Proximity to objective
2. Enemy presence
3. Advantage

TIP

When dropping behind enemy lines and away from your allies, you are on your own. Although other paratroopers may eventually drop in to help, you must survive solo for a while.

SECURE ZONES (SZs)

Each mission has one, two, or even three Secure Zones. These are easy to spot from the air because they are designated with a green smoke grenade. SZs are usually safe places to land because they are often separated from enemy positions by cover. Since SZs are the planned landing spot for paratroopers, that is where crates of supplies are dropped. You can always restore your health to full and fill up your weapons ammo at SZs. Some even have crates of explosives to restock all of your grenades. Finally, SZs are a good place to team up with other paratroopers.

TIP

Secure zones are great places to land when playing a mission for the first time. They offer a chance to get your bearings and take off your chute before you are thrust into a firefight.

SKILL DROPS

Each mission offers you a chance to prove your abilities as a paratrooper with five skill drops. These locations can be identified by a parachute canopy hanging nearby. When you pass by a skill drop, a message appears on the screen, informing you what you must do to complete that skill drop. These range from landing on a church steeple to landing on top of a wall to landing through a doorway. Some skill drops are more difficult to land than others. At the end of each mission, your stats list how many of the five skill drops you were able to complete.

Skill drops are more than just challenging places to land. Just about every one offers some type of advantage. They may be close to an objective, place you in a great spot for sniping down on the enemy below, or offer an alternate route to an objective. For more information on specific skill drops, see the skill drop section in each mission chapter.

TIP

To get all five skill drops for a single mission, you must either wait until you die and jump again into the mission, or land on them when you play the mission over again. When you have landed on a skill drop, it is awarded to you for not only the mission or campaign, but stays with your player profile.

USING THE RIGHT WEAPON

There are several different types of weapons you can use during a mission. As mentioned in The Armory chapter, each weapon as its purpose. Therefore, when engaging the enemy, you can be more combat-effective by using the correct type of weapon.

Tips from the Developer

Weapons become less accurate when moving and turning, and are most accurate when you are motionless and in ironsights. Take advantage of this without spending too much time standing still by learning how to stop and pop—that is, moving around and lining up the shot, then quickly tapping the ironsights button and firing immediately. This is especially important with slow but powerful rifles like the German K98k.

While moving through a building such as a house with small rooms and narrow hallways, a submachine gun or even a shotgun is the weapon of choice. These weapons are not accurate at medium or long range, but their great firepower means you don't have to be as careful about aiming when an enemy surprises you.

Rifles are best used for medium-range targets because they are more accurate. Although they do not have the high rate of fire of a submachine gun, if the enemy is at a distance, you have more time to aim and use cover to make each shot count. Rifles also cause more damage than smaller weapons. As a result, you do not have to get as many hits to kill an enemy.

Automatic rifles can function in combat at both close and medium ranges. Although not as accurate as a rifle at medium range, the automatic rifle's high rate of fire makes up for this. Automatic rifles also have more stopping power than a submachine gun, so when you can pick one of these up, swap it out for that weapon.

Often it is best to engage the enemy at long range where they can't return fire as effectively. For these engagements, a sniper rifle is a must. In fact, as soon as you can get a sniper rifle (in the latter part of Operation Husky), grab one and keep it with you at all times.

The enemy likes to hide behind cover, making it difficult to kill them. That is when you pull out a grenade. Grenades are an indirect weapon. You do not have to be able to see your enemy to use a grenade successfully. When entering a room that you know contains enemies, toss in a grenade first. Because you cannot necessarily see where the enemies are, use your compass to aim. Then throw a grenade so it either bounces off a wall and lands near the enemy, or cook it off and then peek around the doorway to throw it. Even if you don't kill your target, you may force him to run out of the room so you or an ally can kill him with a submachine gun or other weapon. Grenades are also great for killing soldiers manning machine guns.

Tips from the Developer

Two grenades are better than one, so give this a shot. Drop an uncooked grenade at your feet and immediately begin cooking a second grenade. Walk toward the dropped grenade and kick it immediately after throwing your cooked grenade. BOOM-BOOM!

You can pick up and use German stick grenades as well—effectively doubling the total number of grenades you can carry. The German grenades tend to bounce more than the MKII Frag grenades issued by the U.S. Army—especially with long throws, so practice with them a bit to get the feel for the difference between the two types.

USING COVER

Tips from the Developer

Grenades and other explosive weapons will not harm you if you have good cover between yourself and the explosion. Use this to your advantage. A sniper rifle is a good counter to an enemy using an anti-tank weapon if you can learn to use cover effectively. Conversely, if you are using an anti-tank weapon or a grenade against a sniper in hiding, your best bet is to try and hit the ground near him in such a way that his cover will not protect him from the splash damage.

The missions are full of objects that you can hide behind. Since these objects also stop bullets, it is a good idea to use them. The worst thing you can do during a firefight is stand out in the open. You might as well have a big red and white bull's-eye on your chest because that is what you are—a target.

If you want to survive on the battlefield, you have to become an expert at using cover. Even while you are still in the air and getting ready to land, start looking for what you can use for cover if you come under attack right away. On the ground, if enemies are around, you must move from one piece of cover to another. While buildings are considered high cover—they protect you while standing—walls, sandbags and crates are often offer low cover that you must crouch behind for protection.

When moving to cover, always sprint. If you are crouched down behind cover to begin with, use the crouch sprint to get across open ground to the next piece of cover. The faster you move in the open, the less likely the enemy will shoot you. However, to increase your odds even more, fire a few shots or bursts at the enemy and force him to duck down behind cover before you make your sprint. Remember, when behind cover, peek over or lean around the cover when you shoot the enemy rather than standing up or strafing to the side so you expose a smaller part of your body to the enemy.

Tips from the Developer

Save your health! If you are on the verge of losing a bubble of health, run to cover and wait until it is restored. You never know when you are going to need that one bubble between now and your next objective.

FLANKING THE ENEMY

The enemy can be tough to defeat when they set up in a defensive position and behind cover. While you can trade shots at each other from behind cover, there is a better way to fight—flank them.

Flanking works best when you are fighting alongside your allies. They almost always engage the enemy head-on. As a result, they can fix the enemy and possibly suppress them as well. This gives you the opportunity to maneuver to come at the enemy from the side or rear, where you can attack from an angle where they have no cover.

Even if you can't kill them outright, by flanking you may force the enemy to move out from behind their cover because your new approach has now made their position untenable. As a result, your allies may be able to kill the fleeing enemy as they run for new cover.

When flanking an enemy, don't limit yourself to two dimensions. Think like a paratrooper in three dimensions. While you may not be able to move around an enemy while on the ground, using rooftops and other heights may be just the key to finding the flank you can use.

USING ELEVATION

One important aspect designed into each and every mission is what the developers of the game refer to as verticality. Whether it is a rooftop, an upper floor, a small hill, or even a catwalk, you can always find elevated positions. As a paratrooper, you can often choose to begin in such locations by landing there in the first place. In almost all circumstances, you gain an advantage with the high ground.

Not only do rooftops and upper levels often offer a way to get around the enemy's defenses and possibly flank them, firing from a height advantage can essentially be a flanking attack. They lose the protection of their cover when you are positioned above them because your line of fire reaches over the top of their cover rather than being blocked, as it would be if you were on the same level. This is also true when using grenades. Rather than having to lob a grenade over an obstacle, you can just drop grenades right on top of your enemies.

In addition to gaining an offensive advantage over lower enemies, you also gain a defensive advantage, because anything you use as cover is now more effective when an enemy below tries to attack you. Therefore, when up high, crouch down so the enemy can't shoot you, then peek down to fire—even if your only cover is the peak of a rooftop or an edge of an upper level.

Tips from the Developer

Keep your eyes peeled for pathways back to the rooftops or other heights. If you did not take the opportunity to land on the rooftops on your initial descent, you can still get back to the roof via ladders and stairs. If a particular encounter is posing a significant problem, rise above it.

GEORGE MARSHALL AND TACTICS

As the head of the Infantry School at Fort Benning during the late 1920s and early 1930s, George Marshall, who would later become the Army chief of staff and general during WWII, wanted to prepare the U.S. Army for the next war. Having served in the First World War, Marshall saw the carnage resulting from frontal attacks on enemy trenches. While other armies were developing volumes of tactics for every conceivable situation, Marshall wanted something simple. He knew that during another war, the U.S. Army would be made up of mostly draftees taken right out of civilian life. There would not be a lot of time to train these men how to be soldiers, let alone teach them a vast number of tactics. What if they needed to be taught only a single tactic?

Marshall decided that the Infantry School would teach only one tactic—the holding attack. Taught in only five minutes, the holding attack could be used in any situation. Terrain, force size, weather—none of these mattered. The tactic was always the same. First you sent part of your force to advance on the enemy and engage, pinning down the enemy and preventing them from maneuvering. Then another part of the force maneuvered around the enemy to hit them in the flank or rear. Additional forces, if available, could be held in reserve to help out either of the two forces, depending on the results of the attack. Armed with a single, all-purpose tactic, American soldiers, from generals to sergeants, could focus on implementing the tactic rather than determining which tactic to use.

Marshall simplified the Army's training and made it more relevant to the battlefields of the twentieth century. This was in reaction to the methods of World War I, which reflected warfare of the nineteenth century. To help impart this information, Marshall was instrumental in the publishing of *Infantry in Battle*. This military text used examples from World War I to illustrate key military principles—all of which had been studied, analyzed, and tested at the Infantry School. As a result of Marshall's foresight and that of other young officers (such as Matthew Ridgeway who later commanded the 82nd Airborne Division) during the interwar years, the American soldier was better trained to think on his own during battle rather than wait for instructions from his superiors. This was not true for the soldiers of other countries.

If you would like to read *Infantry in Battle*, an electronic copy is available on the U.S. Army's Command and General Staff website at http://cgsc.leavenworth.army.mil/carl/resources/csi/iib_iji/iib_iji.asp#416.

ENEMY TACTICS

To understand the tactics the enemy uses against you, you first need to appreciate how the enemy artificial intelligence (AI) thinks. Since this game is an open, sandbox-style game rather than the typical linear shooter, its AI is different. In linear games, the AI can be scripted for each engagement because the player always comes from a specific direction and must move through a defined area. Since you can drop into a mission pretty much anywhere, select which objectives you want to go after first, and even from which direction you want to attack, scripting the enemy AI would not work. Instead, a new system was developed to allow the AI to react to the your actions, which could be different each time.

TIP

The enemy detects threats—such as you—in three different ways. First, if an enemy sees you, it will then begin attacking. The second way is by sound. If you are running, you make a lot more noise than when you are moving slowly while crouched. The more noise you make, the more likely it is that the enemy will detect you—and at longer ranges. Finally, when you fire at the enemy, it automatically realize there is a threat. That is why after you take a long range shot with a sniper rifle, those enemies close to the bullet's path, or near the enemy you killed, will take cover. Therefore, when trying to flank an enemy, go low and slow, and make sure you aim carefully with your first shot.

The Affordance Engine was the solution. It basically uses the same system a real commander on the battlefield would use to make decisions—affordances. An affordance is a feature of the immediate environment that offers some type of advantage. For example, a rooftop provides a better view and larger area of fire for a soldier. A wall provides a defense against enemy fire. However, an upper floor of a building would offer both of these affordances—increased attack ability as well as increased defense. In real life, a commander would order his troops to move into positions where they could maximize their affordance against the enemy while minimizing the enemy's affordance against them. The same goes for the game's enemy AI.

Let's take a look at how this works in the game: While advancing toward an objective, you come across a group of enemies. When they detect you, or you attack them, the enemy soldiers return fire and move to cover because that provides a defensive advantage to them. If a machine gun position is not occupied, a soldier may move to the gun and man it because it provides a firepower advantage as well as a defensive advantage (since the machine gun has sandbags around it).

If you just stay hidden behind cover, some of the enemy may begin to advance on your position. Since you are not firing and threatening them, they try to gain an offensive advantage over you while moving away from their defensive advantage—their cover. If possible, they try to move into a position to reduce your defensive advantage and flank you.

Now, you peek up over your cover and begin firing on the advancing enemies, killing some of them. As you become more of a threat, the rest seek cover. As you begin to advance around to one side to flank them, the enemy realizes they are losing their defensive advantage and begin to move to new cover that can protect them against attacks from your new position. As a result, the engagement becomes very fluid.

NOTE

The Affordance Engine even controls the way the enemy reacts to a grenade you throw at them. The grenade represents a big threat, so they quickly move to get away and find cover that can protect them from the grenade. However, if you throw the grenade too short and it lands on the opposite side of cover from the enemy, they will stay put since the cover they have will protect them.

As a result of your flanking maneuver, you are able to kill several of the enemies. Your allies (fellow paratroopers) are advancing forward along with you. The few remaining enemies now realize they are outnumbered and at a disadvantage. As a result, they withdraw, moving away from the engagement and stopping to take cover where they once again have an advantage, as this new position shelters other enemy soldiers as well.

Feeling confident, you rush after the enemies and end up wounded. Your allies are also getting hammered. As you return to an SZ to restore your health and your allies are killed, the enemy realizes they can advance back to the original position since the threats there have decreased.

That example shows the basics of how the Affordance Engine works. As you go up against more elite enemies, you will notice they act a bit differently. They tend to be more aggressive and charge at you more. This is because they have more firepower and can take more damage. Because they already have an advantage, they advance. If you represent a bigger threat by firing at them with an automatic weapon at close range, they will then tend to take cover.

Now that you have an understanding of the Affordance Engine, how can you use this information? The key is always to seek to minimize the enemy's affordances. If they have cover, get them to move out of it by flanking them or throwing a grenade over the top of the cover. Climb up on a rooftop to reduce the effectiveness of their cover. Fire at the enemy to pin them down behind cover so you or your allies can advance without taking fire. While this may seem academic now, as you play through the missions and observe the enemy, you will see the enemy react to your actions by trying to maximize their advantages and minimize yours.

Tips from the Developer

You do not need to hit your target to be combat-effective. Any enemy who takes cover can be pinned in place from suppressing fire. Use an automatic weapon to fire a long burst in the opponent's general direction, then move around to his flank to finish him off.

USING YOUR ALLIES

When you drop into a mission, other paratroopers are dropping along with you. Airborne troops were trained to work as a team. If you try to go it alone, leaving your allies behind, you will find the missions to be much more challenging. Therefore, work with your allies, letting them help you as you help them in turn.

Tips from the Developer

When fighting alongside a group of allies, observe their movements and try to stay with them as they advance. Do not push too far ahead of the group, either, as you may find yourself stranded without helpful suppressing fire if your allies die.

Your allies use the same Affordance Engine as the enemies. They seek to increase their advantages while decreasing those of the enemy. However, the airborne troops have something the enemy does not—you. Without you, your allies can't advance to an objective on their own. They need your help to clear out the enemies so they can move forward to the next position.

While you cannot directly control your allies, you can work with them. During an engagement, they fire at the enemy and kill some of them while you do the same, helping you to clear out the enemy. The other advantage of sticking with your allies is the enemy must divide their fire between you and your allies. If you are on your own, every enemy you encounter is firing at you.

Your allies can also warn you of danger or request your help. During a firefight, if you have the enemy pinned behind cover, a paratrooper may say, "Travers, cover me" (your character is Boyd Travers). The paratrooper then rushes toward the enemy. If you lay down suppressing fire to force the enemy to keep their heads down, your ally can move around the enemy's cover to flank and kill them. However, if you just duck behind your cover, most likely your ally will be killed.

Tips from the Developer

Keep an ear open to your allies' chatter. Your friendly squad members can point out grenades, enemy reinforcements, or friendly losses. If your allies call out to advance, support them with suppressing fire or charge ahead with them. Your allies will hold territory for you, but only if you are vigilant about ensuring their survival as well as your own.

The best way to observe how your allies function is during Operation Husky. As you advance through the gate and into the hilltop houses, where the first machine gun is at the end of the street next to a halftrack, leave your allies in the street and head up to the gatehouse. Fire your rifle out the window at the enemies below. As you begin to clear them out, especially those manning the machine gun, watch as your allies begin to advance to man the machine gun themselves and begin to clear out the house on the left. They then continue to advance to the next engagement. This tactic of staying back and supporting your allies is even more effective when you have a sniper rifle.

DEVELOP YOUR OWN TACTICS

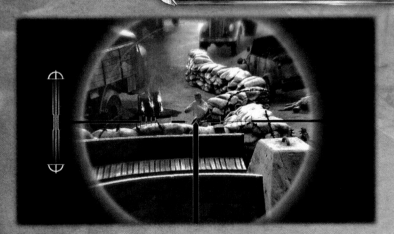

This game offers a lot of flexibility for the player. Each mission can be completed in a number of different ways. There is no single way to play. If you like being a sniper, find good spots from which you can fire on the enemy below and help clear the way for your allies to advance. On the other hand, if you like to be in the middle of the action, grab a submachine gun or even a shotgun. For this type of fighting, you must be good at using cover. Develop your own tactics that reflect your style of play. Experiment with different ways of playing. The more you play each of the missions, the more you will appreciate and enjoy this game.

OPERATION HUSKY

WAR & NAVY
DEPARTMENTS
V-MAIL SERVICE

OFFICIAL BUSINESS

U.S. POSTAL SERVICE NO. 2
JUN 10
3-PM
1944

PENALTY FOR PRIVATE USE TO AVOID
PAYMENT OF POSTAGE, $300

OPERATION HUSKY
Italy

The object of war is not to die for
your country but to make the
other bastard die for his.
—General George S. Patton

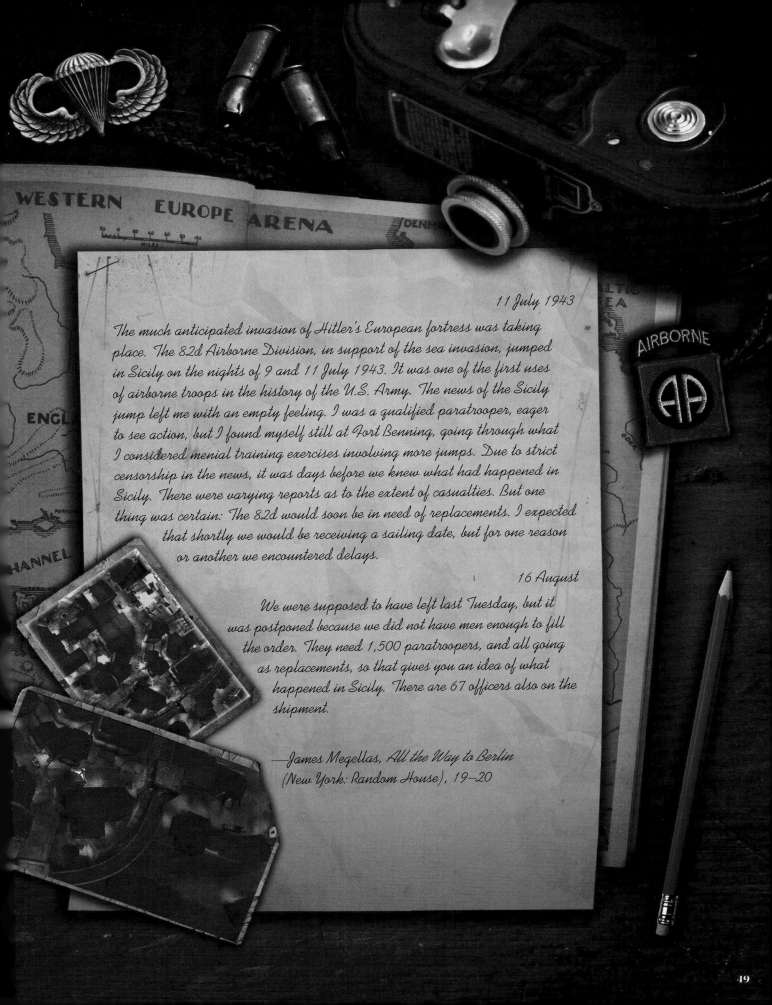

11 July 1943

The much anticipated invasion of Hitler's European fortress was taking place. The 82d Airborne Division, in support of the sea invasion, jumped in Sicily on the nights of 9 and 11 July 1943. It was one of the first uses of airborne troops in the history of the U.S. Army. The news of the Sicily jump left me with an empty feeling. I was a qualified paratrooper, eager to see action, but I found myself still at Fort Benning, going through what I considered menial training exercises involving more jumps. Due to strict censorship in the news, it was days before we knew what had happened in Sicily. There were varying reports as to the extent of casualties. But one thing was certain: The 82d would soon be in need of replacements. I expected that shortly we would be receiving a sailing date, but for one reason or another we encountered delays.

16 August

We were supposed to have left last Tuesday, but it was postponed because we did not have men enough to fill the order. They need 1,500 paratroopers, and all going as replacements, so that gives you an idea of what happened in Sicily. There are 67 officers also on the shipment.

—James Megellas, *All the Way to Berlin*
(New York: Random House), 19–20

MEDAL OF HONOR
AIRBORNE

Briefing

As a part of the invasion of Sicily, your unit will be dropping into the town of Adanti with orders to secure it from the enemies and prevent them from using it as a staging area for counterattacks against Allied amphibious landings on the coast. You must first neutralize the antiaircraft emplacements in the town and then drive out the enemy.

Hamlet

Northeast
Gate

Church

Market

Market
Plaza

Hill Houses

Southwest
Residence

Tower
Plaza

Town
Hall

LEGEND

Objectives

- 🏳️ Destroy Hill Houses' AA Gun
- 🏳️ Destroy Northeast Gate's AA Gun
- 🏳️ Destroy Town Hall's AA Guns
- 🏳️ Assemble with Airborne at North Gate
- 🏳️ Locate Missing Sniper Team
- 🏳️ Eliminate German Commander
- 🏳️ Assemble with Airborne at Town Square
- 🏳️ Eliminate 3 German Officers

Secure Zones
(inside light green overlay)

- 🏳️ Behind Church
- 🏳️ Tower Plaza

Skill Drops

- 1️⃣ Land through the gatehouse window
- 2️⃣ Land on the balcony through the opening
- 3️⃣ Stick the landing on the church steeple
- 4️⃣ Land on the small rooftop
- 5️⃣ Land on the catwalk inside the tower

Weapon Pickups

- 🔫 Springfield Sniper Rifle
- 🔫 Machine Gun Positions
- ➕ Health

Miscellaneous

- 📋 Ladder

Weapon Loadout

- M1928 Thompson
- M1 Garand
- M1911 Colt .45

ADANTI

Operation Husky

History

Following success in North Africa, the Allies continued operations in the Mediterranean Theatre. Winston Churchill, the British Prime Minister, viewed Italy as "the soft underbelly" of the Nazi crocodile. However, in order to invade the Italian peninsula, the Allies would need a base of operations closer than North Africa. The island of Sicily, located just off the coast of the "toe" of the Italian "boot," was chosen as the prelude to the invasion of Italy.

Allied infantry divisions would be hitting the shore on the morning of July 10, 1943. To help support them, British and U.S. paratroops were dropped the night before to act as roadblocks to slow down Italian and German forces moving to the beaches to repel the Allied landings. While there had been some smaller airborne drops during Operation Torch—the invasion of North Africa—Husky would be the first major Allied airborne operation. Due to the limited number of aircraft, only the 505th Parachute Infantry Regiment (PIR) from the U.S. 82nd Airborne Division would make a drop that first night along with the 3rd Battalion, 504th PIR. They would support the U.S. landings while the British 1st Airborne Division would support the British landings.

Since many of the pilots carrying the paratroopers had little experience flying in formation at night with only a quarter moon providing very little light, the drop started to fall apart before the transport planes were even close to Sicily. As a result, only 20 percent of the paratroopers landed somewhere near their drop zones. Others were scattered—some were up to 65 miles away! General James Gavin, the airborne troop commander for this drop, was not even sure if he was in Sicily when he hit the ground. However, a few units were able to assemble and move on their objectives. The rest of the paratroopers acted on their own, causing as much confusion as possible and doing what they could to tie up enemy troops. In fact, the wide dispersion of paratroops actually slowed down the Italian response to the invasion because the commanders were getting reports of paratroopers all over southeastern Sicily and did not know where to concentrate their forces. Although the paratroopers were not able to achieve all of their objectives, they did slow down the enemy counterattack enough so that the Allied infantry could get ashore and establish a beachhead.

SECURE THE TOWN OF ADANTI

Your first objectives are to neutralize the enemy AA guns in Adanti. There are four of them in three different locations. Two are on top of the town hall, one is in the southwest in the area known as the hill houses, and the last is outside of the northeast gate of the town. However, the town is defended by Italian Blackshirt troops—and they will not let you blow up their guns without a fight.

LANDING IN ADANTI

The drop zone for this mission is anywhere within the town walls. There are two established secure zones—one near the church and the other in the tower plaza. There are no enemies near these SZs, so you can safely land here without the threat of being shot while trying to get out of your parachute. You can also find containers with health and ammo at each of these SZs.

Jump out of your plane. The town of Adanti lies below you.

It does not matter which AA guns you go after first. As you move toward one, your allies follow and help you out. The best time to determine your first objective is before you jump out of the plane. Your objective determines where you want to try to land. The skill drop locations are usually good places to begin. However, any rooftop will do. As a paratrooper, you must think of the battlefield in three dimensions, and Adanti has a lot of heights. Use the rooftops to your advantage. If you miss a rooftop, there are a few ladders around the town that provide access to the rooftops in the market and tower plaza areas.

Landing on the rooftops can give you a height advantage over the enemy— allowing you to fire down on them. You can even use the rooftops to get around enemy positions to hit their flanks.

Tips from the Developer

Land on the roof of the church to provide vertical cover for your allies in the street fight below. When they move up through the gate, stay on the roof. As the allies enter the first section of the hill houses, you can engage the enemies by firing over the top of the city wall.

—Rex Dickson

SKILL DROPS

There are five skill drop locations in Adanti. Each provides some advantage as you move to achieve your objectives of taking out the AA guns. Some are easier to get than others.

The first skill drop is one of the toughest. You must land through the northeast gatehouse window. While still up high in the air, line yourself up with the window so you are dropping right next to it. As you get near, flare and push toward the window to drop right through. From this position in the gatehouse, you can help your paratroopers below advance on the gatehouse, and then help them clear out the courtyard on the other side.

The second skill drop location can be found to the side of the town hall. It faces a courtyard and you must land on the balcony as you drop through the arch. This one is not too tough to hit. There is a soldier on the balcony that you must take out. Then you can advance toward the town hall, taking up a flanking position against the enemy troops out in front.

While the church steeple might seem like a simple place to land, the key is to stick the landing. There is not a lot of space on top and it is easy to over- or undershoot the landing. The steeple provides a great vantage point for taking out the enemy troops below near the western gate leading to the hill houses. Use your rifle to help clear the way for your fellow paratroopers. You can even drop some grenades from this location.

The last skill drop location is the tower near the town hall. You must land on the catwalk inside the roofless tower. Because an enemy soldier is there, you have to take him out quickly. Try aiming to land right on top of him, and then pressing the melee button just as you are about to hit him. This eliminates the soldier and clears the top of the tower. From here you can fire through the window at the enemies below in front of the town hall. Another enemy soldier is in the tower a few flights down, so you might want to kill him before you start firing away at the enemies below.

The small rooftop is another tough landing to stick. It is located near the market courtyard. Landing here allows you to quickly access the rooftops overlooking the northeast gate as well as the town hall. From these heights, you can help your allies clear out the enemies so you can advance to the AA guns.

DESTROY THE HILL HOUSES' AA GUN

There is no particular order in which you must destroy the AA guns. Don't feel like you have to use the order in this chapter. You may want to take out the town hall guns first and then go after the other two. The choice is up to you.

LEGEND

 Machine Gun Positions   **Health**

Miscellaneous

📖 **Ladder**   ← **Recommended Path**

Weapon Loadout

- M1928 Thompson
- M1911 Colt .45
- M1 Garand

If the hill house AA guns are your first objective, then a good place to land is on top of the church. Try for the steeple if possible. However, if you can't stick the landing, any part of the church rooftop is just as good. Blackshirt troops take up positions in front of the western gatehouse when your troops begin to engage them. There is also a single Blackshirt soldier inside the gatehouse. Since it does not have a roof, throw a grenade into the gatehouse to take him out. If you let the grenade cook for a couple of seconds before throwing, the enemy soldier does not have time to get away before the grenade goes off.

Destroy the gate house guard with a grenade.

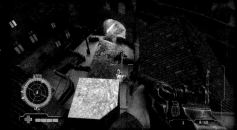

The church steeple or roof make a great place for sniping the enemy below.

Next use your M1 Garand to begin picking off Blackshirts down on the road below. Be sure to crouch down to make yourself a harder target for them to hit. Also try throwing some grenades down on them. Just be sure to let the grenades cook off for about three seconds or the enemy will scatter. Move along the roofline toward the gatehouse to hit the enemies from the sides and deny them cover. As you clear them out, your paratrooper brothers advance to the archway through the gatehouse.

Advance through the archway to the hill house area.

Don't drop down to the street just yet. You can still take out some of the enemies on the other side of the gatehouse from the church rooftop. At the far end of the street, Blackshirts man a machine gun. If you are a good shot, you can take out these gunners and give your allies a fighting chance to move forward to secure this area. Eventually you want to step off the rooftop to get down to ground level. Be sure to pick up any ammo left behind by the Italians. For this part, switch to your Thompson submachine gun because you will be engaging the enemy at a closer range.

Move through the archway and use the cover on each side of the street as you engage the enemy. Crouch down and then pop up while in ironsights view to shoot. Fire a few bursts and then duck back down again. The

Use the Garand to kill the machine gunner at long range.

mounted machine gun at the end of the street is still your main threat. Use grenades to eliminate the enemy manning it. Advance along the right side of the street in short rushes before the machine gun is manned by another enemy. Blackshirt reinforcements arrive through the house (house 1) on the left, as well as from around the corner on the left.

This halftrack can provide cover for you as you head to the machine gun.

Work your way to the halftrack on the right side and use it for cover from the enemy fire coming from the house. Peek around the rear of the halftrack and eliminate the latest machine gunner. From this angle on the machine gun's flank, you can hit the gunner, but he can't hit you. Stay here and keep the Blackshirts away from the machine gun until one of your allies can man it.

Tips from the Developer

Look for a fallen rain gutter on the left about halfway down the street. You can use it to get up onto the rooftop. From there, you can fire down on the enemies below.

—Rex Dickson

Now that the first street is secure, it is time to advance again. House 1 contains a health kit, so pick it up if you need it as well as any ammo lying around. You need to keep up the pressure or the Blackshirts will try to push you back. Head down the street toward the house (house 2) south of the machine gun. Approach it from the right side and use the side doorway for cover as you clear out the Italians inside. Wait for some allies to catch up to you before moving in.

Clear out this room in house 2, then use it for cover.

You can use the short stone wall behind the house from the first street for cover as you engage enemies along the north-south street. However, the machine gun at the south end of the street can make this position difficult to hold.

Make your way across the room to the opposite doorway, using it for cover as you engage any Blackshirts on the other side. More of them will be coming from the south end of the street. There is also another machine gun at the end of this street—on the left-hand side. As before, wait for some of your allies to catch up before you push on ahead. The enemies keep coming, so once you have some fellow paratroopers to help provide cover, move out along the right side of the street. Use a grenade to silence the machine gun and the work your way to the short wall at the corner of the house. From this vantage, you can see move Blackshirts down the east-west street to your right.

Rush up these steps and into the southern half of house 2. This allows you to get to the objective and avoid a lot of enemy firepower.

At the end of the street, which climbs up a short hill, the enemy have positioned two machine guns to guard their AA gun. Advancing up the street would be suicide. Therefore, sprint around the corner of the house and then up the short stairs on the street's right side and enter another part of house 2, picking up the health by the doorway if you need it. After making sure the room is clear, cautiously head up the stairs to the second floor. Watch your compass to see if there are any enemies to your left when you get to the top of the stairs. Eliminate any Blackshirts to clear this room, and then head through the doorway near the stairs. The house allows you to get to the top of the hill without taking fire from the two machine guns.

Exit the house and begin clearing out the area around the AA gun.

From the safety of the house, begin taking out Blackshirts. You can use the back doorway for cover and can even eliminate a soldier manning one of the machine guns from this spot, giving your allies a better chance to get to the top of the hill. After clearing out all the enemies you can see, quickly move through the doorway to take cover behind the stone walls and sandbags. Once behind cover, proceed with caution as you clear out the hilltop one enemy at a time. They hide behind the walls and sandbags as well, so keep your weapon topped off and be ready to perform a melee attack if a Blackshirt jumps out and rushes you.

TIP

Take out the soldier on the second machine gun in order to get more of your paratroopers up the hill to help you clear it of enemies.

Place a charge on the AA gun to complete this objective.

Work your way along the northern part of the hilltop area while you face toward the south. When you get to the western edge, begin moving south. Continue past the AA gun toward the small building and ensure that it is clear of enemies as well. By this time, your allies should have joined up with you and the hilltop should now be secure. Return to the AA gun, place an explosive charge on it, and then move away before it detonates.

You have to fight your way back to the West Gate.

Now that this objective is completed, move back to the center of the town. Pick up ammo and health along the way. However, as you approach house 1, be ready for action. Some Blackshirts have taken up positions near the gatehouse. Use the machine gun at the end of the street to mow them down, or let one of your allies man it while you advance up one side of the street, clearing your way as you go.

DESTROY THE NORTHEAST GATE'S AA GUN

Antiair Gun

House

Gate House

PRIMA Official Game Guide ... 58 ... Gatehouse

LEGEND

⊟ Machine Gun Positions ✚ Health

Miscellaneous

📒 Ladder ⟵ Recommended Path

Weapon Loadout

• M1928 Thompson • M1911 Colt .45
• M1 Garand

The Market building also offers some great elevated positions from which to fire down on the Blackshirts guarding the gatehouse archway, including balconies, windows, and even a rooftop access from one of the balconies. However, several enemies are inside this building as well. You can skip this building altogether and just go for the objective. However, if you want to get some additional kills and try to earn some upgrades for your weapons, be sure to clear out this building. Just be careful as you move from room to room. The Blackshirts are usually hiding behind cover such as overturned tables and other furniture.

This ladder near the northeast gate gets you up to the rooftops.

This objective isn't quite as involved as the hill house's AA gun. If you are dropping into this objective, try to get the skill drop for either the gatehouse or the small rooftop. The key is to stay up high as much as possible. If you are coming from another objective and are already on the ground, there is a ladder to the west of the gatehouse that allows you access to the rooftops.

From the rooftops, you have a great shot at the enemies below.

Take out the soldier on the machine gun before he gets you.

From the rooftops, you can fire down on the enemy soldiers below. They gather outside the archway to block your entrance into the objective area. Your allies take up positions to the south and begin to engage the Blackshirts. After thinning out some of the enemy, advance onto the city wall and continue to the gatehouse. Be very careful while in the gatehouse. There is a machine gun in the second floor of the house to the northeast. Since it can hit you in the gatehouse, even while you are crouched, be sure to snipe the gunner first before turning around and attacking the Blackshirts out in front of the archway so your allies can advance to help you.

Take out the Germans down in the courtyard.

Head up these stairs so you can clear
out the area around the AA gun.

When the front of the archway is clear, shift your fire to
the courtyard on the other side. Watch the machine gun
because Blackshirts occasionally try to use it to fire on
you and your troops. When the courtyard is clear, you can
actually jump through the gatehouse window down into the
courtyard. Advance along the walkway on the right side,
picking up some health and ammo along the way, and enter
the house. After making sure the first floor is clear, go
upstairs to clear out the second floor. Move to the back
windows; they give you a great spot from which to fire down
on the Blackshirts guarding the AA gun below.

A well-thrown
grenade blows up
two Germans in the
side building.

Some Blackshirts may try to hole up in the building off to
the right of the AA gun. Try to kill them from the second
floor windows by throwing grenades through the door. If
that does not kill them, your allies might be able to do it
when they run out of the building. Go back down the stairs
and around to the area where the AA gun is located. Check
your compass to make sure you got all of the enemies. If
some are still in the small building, finish them off with a
grenade or by rushing in and using your Thompson.

When the area is
clear, move to the
AA gun and place a
charge to destroy it.
Pick up health and
ammo as you head
back to the archway
and exit this area.
No enemies try to
stop you, so you can
then proceed to your
next objective.

One more AA gun to destroy.

TIP

During this mission, it is
possible to earn all three
upgrades for the Thompson
submachine gun. However,
rather than continuing to use
this powerful weapon, switch
to an enemy MP40 submachine
gun and start working toward upgrading it. You can also upgrade
the M1 Garand rifle at least once during this mission. The key to
earning upgrades is patience. Sit back and eliminate enemies as
they appear. You also earn more points for upgrades by making
headshots or using your weapon for melee attacks.

DESTROY THE TOWN HALL'S AA GUNS

LEGEND

Miscellaneous

Weapon Loadout

Machine Gun Positions   Health   Ladder   ← Recommended Path

- M1928 Thompson
- M1 Garand
- M1911 Colt .45

The town hall is well defended.

The town hall has two AA guns mounted on its rooftop. There are several ways to go about completing this objective. The toughest by far is the frontal assault from the street. Try to avoid that method altogether. If you are jumping into the battle, you can land in the tower to achieve a skill drop. An enemy soldier is right there, so you need to take him out. Then descend a few flights of stairs to eliminate a second Blackshirt. From the tower windows, you can fire down on the enemy below as they try to prevent your allies from getting into the town hall.

The tower provides a good spot for sniping the Blackshirts on the rooftop of the town hall, as well as in front of it.

Move through the alleys in the southwestern part of the city to get to the basement entrance to the town hall.

The western side of the town hall offers a safer way to enter the building. There is a basement entrance next to the city wall. You must eliminate some soldiers in the alleyways leading to this entrance, as well as some who might be hiding out in the basement. However, once it is clear, you can take the stairs up to the first floor, where you (usually) come in behind the enemy in the room on the western side. This is the best place to enter at ground level since the main entrance is covered by a machine gun at the top of the central stairway.

TIP

If you are really daring, try to drop right onto the top of the town hall. It is safer to land near the rear, where you can find some cover quickly. Try to clear out the Blackshirts on the roof's western side while also watching for reinforcements coming up the stairs on the eastern side. If you can clear enough enemies, paratroopers start to drop in to help you. Then blow up the AA guns. Because you did not clear the town hall, you must fight the Blackshirts inside the building on your way out. Or, you can jump over the eastern or western sides, landing on the rooftops, which you can take to your next objective—bypassing the town hall interior entirely.

Clear out this western room on the first floor.

Clear out this room, whether you are coming in from the front or basement, and then approach the doorway to the foyer. Clear out this room, and then make your way along the right side of the room, up the stairs, and on toward the machine gun. Throw a grenade to kill the gunner and then rush up the rest of the stairway to take a position near the machine gun. Don't man it—instead concentrate on eliminating Blackshirts headed in your direction. An ally usually mans the gun for you and helps provide cover fire as you advance down the walkway to the right along the eastern side of the room.

Rush up the side of the central staircase to take out the soldier manning the machine gun at the top.

You can avoid the first floor altogether. Get up onto the city wall. There are stairs near the western gate. As you approach the town hall, hop up onto the rooftops. Continue moving toward the town hall and locate the open window. Clear the room before entering. Once inside, take up a position near the doorway and clear out the next room, where some Blackshirts are hiding behind cover. You can now move out to engage the machine gun and continue on from there.

Stay crouched and watch for enemies ahead of you. Some come through the doorways on your right sides. Skip the boarded up doorway and continue to the second doorway. The Blackshirts inside are taking cover behind an overturned table. Throw a grenade in to make them move, and then peek around the doorway to blast away with your Thompson. Use your compass to see if the room is clear before entering it. Continue on to the next room and clear it of any enemies remain.

Move down this walkway with your allies.

Clear the area at the rear of the town hall roof.

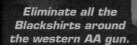

Eliminate all the Blackshirts around the western AA gun.

It is now time to go up to the roof. Take the stairs to the southeast corner of the roof. Wait for some paratroopers to join you and then begin taking out the Italians on the roof. It is sometimes easier to work your way around the back of the roof. Use the crates for cover as you advance and clear the roof's western side. Don't worry about blowing up the AA gun yet. Continue toward the front of the building and use your guns and grenades to take out the remaining Blackshirts near the eastern AA gun. Many enemies are up here, and the fighting can be really close, so stay alert and take your time, moving from cover to cover. After all the enemies on the rooftop have been eliminated, pick up any ammo and health you might need and then set charges on both AA guns to complete this objective.

Blow up the AA guns on the roof.

Go back down to the ground level. Stay alert for Blackshirts as you move back through the town hall. You may have missed some on your way up—or bypassed them when you entered the building at a higher level. Now continue on to another objective.

Tips from the Developer

When dropping into Husky, position yourself over top of the balcony of the town hall, overlooking the town square. As you approach the MG gunner on the balcony, press the melee button to drop kick him on the way in. You can now use this position to rain machine gun fire down on the enemies in the town square. This position also gives you immediate access to the second floor interior of the town hall.

—Rex Dickson

THE NORTH GATE

ASSEMBLE WITH THE AIRBORNE AT THE NORTH GATE

Your first three objectives are complete. Now you get some new orders.

During a mission, if you ever need to fully restore your health, or restock all your ammo, head for a secure zone. They are designated by green smoke and offer crates of ammo and health.

Move out to the north gate.

After you have destroyed all four AA guns, make your way to the north gate of the town. By this time, the town is pretty clear, so you should have no trouble getting there.

NOTE

After the AA guns have been silenced, when you die, you will no longer respawn up in the air. Instead, you will find yourself on the streets of Adanti.

LOCATE THE MISSING SNIPER TEAM

Sniper
Team

German
Commander

North
Gate

LEGEND

Miscellaneous

 Machine Gun Positions   Health   Ladder   ← Recommended Path

Weapon Loadout

• M1928 Thompson

• M1 Garand

• M1911 Colt .45

Upon meeting up with the Airborne at the north gate, a grenade detonates and you will receive new orders. It seems a sniper team has been cut off and your job is to go find them. In addition to these orders, you also learn that German Heer infantry has moved into town. These soldiers put up more of a fight and are tougher than the Blackshirts, so be ready for more intense action. Down the street from your position, a German machine gun opens up on you. In order to advance along with your fellow paratroopers, you must silence that gun.

Rush across the street to this building.

Rather than trying to advance down the street, sprint across the street and enter the building through the open door. Ascend the stairs and then move out onto the balcony. Turn right and hop up onto the rooftop. From here, throw a grenade to take out the gunner below. Let it cook off for about three seconds and throw it so it bounces off the wall across the road and drops right next to the machine gun. Engage other Germans below until your paratroops can advance to the machine gun position and then on toward the objective.

Take out the machine gunner with one of your grenades.

Do as much damage as you can from the rooftop, then drop down to the street level. Enter the building to the north and clear it out. Watch for enemies hiding behind cover. Advance through the

Germans like to hide in this building.

house and begin firing on the enemy while in the northern room. As you can, move to the doorway, using it for cover, and eliminate all enemies on the right side of the courtyard. Then try to shoot the soldier manning the machine gun in the second building across the way. Use the M1 Garand since you need some accuracy to hit the only part of the solider exposed—his head.

After the machine gunner is killed, move into the courtyard and fire on the enemies to your left. Continue advancing toward the building with the machine gun, clearing away enemies as you go. There is some health

The sniper team is on the second floor of this building.

in the building if you need it. When the room is clear, walk up the stairs to meet the sniper team.

ELIMINATE THE GERMAN COMMANDER

You have found the sniper team—though they are not in very good shape.

When you get to the top of the stairs, you find one of the snipers dead and the other wounded. He informs you of a German commander in another building who is calling in reinforcements to take back Adanti. Since the surviving sniper is unable to use the rifle, it is up to you to kill the German commander. Crouch down and walk over to the sniper rifle. Switch to your M1, and then swap it for the Springfield sniper rifle.

Line up your shot on the German Commander.

Move over to the window and bring up the scope view just like you would your ironsights. It takes a second for your sight to focus. Then peek up over the window sill and locate the enemy inside another building. Zoom in your scope if necessary, place the crosshairs over the head of the commander, and then fire. The enemy commander w be firing at you, so don't take too long. The German appear randomly at one of three windows and will change positions frequently. When you have killed him, one more objective is complete.

REPEL THE ENEMY COUNTERATTACK

ASSEMBLE WITH THE AIRBORNE AT THE TOWN SQUARE

Use your sniper rifle to clear the way back to the town square.

Hold onto the Springfield sniper rifle because you can use it for the next part of the mission. Go back down the stairs and make your way down the street toward the first machine gun position. Germans have taken up a position at the end of the street, near the north gate. Hide behind cover and use the sniper rifle to clear them out. You must move down the street, using crates and walls for cover. The building on the left side also provides cover, allowing you to shoot through windows so you can get the right angle for a shot on the enemies. After they have all been neutralized, advance through the north gate, then continue on toward the town square.

ELIMINATE THE THREE GERMAN OFFICERS

There is a battle for the town hall.

By the time you reach the town square, German reinforcements have rolled in and taken over the town hall. The German infantry is positioned around the front of the building. You also receive new orders. Three German officers in the town hall must be eliminated. All three are in the western part of the building, but on different floors. One is on the first floor, another is on the second floor, and the last is on the roof.

Now that you have a sniper rifle, this is a perfect opportunity to earn an upgrade for it. Climb up the ladder along the street so you can get up to the rooftops. Position yourself behind the crest of the roof so you can crouch down and not be seen. Then pop up and begin picking off Germans. Start with the machine gunner on the balcony and then work your way down. There are enough enemies out in front for you to collect your first sniper rifle upgrade—a polished match grade bolt that increases your rate of fire.

You can choose how you want to enter the town hall. If you clear out all the soldiers in front, you can go in through the front door on the right. However, you can bypass those soldiers and enter either though the basement or the second floor window as mentioned earlier in this chapter. The German soldiers take up similar positions to the Blackshirts you mopped up earlier. Watch out for the machine gun at the top of the central staircase. Your compass helps you locate not only enemies, but also the target German officers. Advance through the town hall along with your allies and kill all the officers. When all three are dead, the mission is complete—even if you have not mopped up the rest of the German soldiers.

This officer is on the first floor.

The next officer is in the room directly above on the second floor.

The last German officer is on the roof near the western AA gun.

OPERATION AVALANCHE

WAR & NAVY
DEPARTMENTS
V–MAIL SERVICE

OFFICIAL BUSINESS

PENALTY FOR PRIVATE USE TO AVOID
PAYMENT OF POSTAGE. $300

US POSTAL SERVICE NO.2
JUN 10
3-PM
1944

OPERATION AVALANCHE
Italy

Veni, vidi, vici. (I came, I saw,
I conquered.)

—Julius Caesar

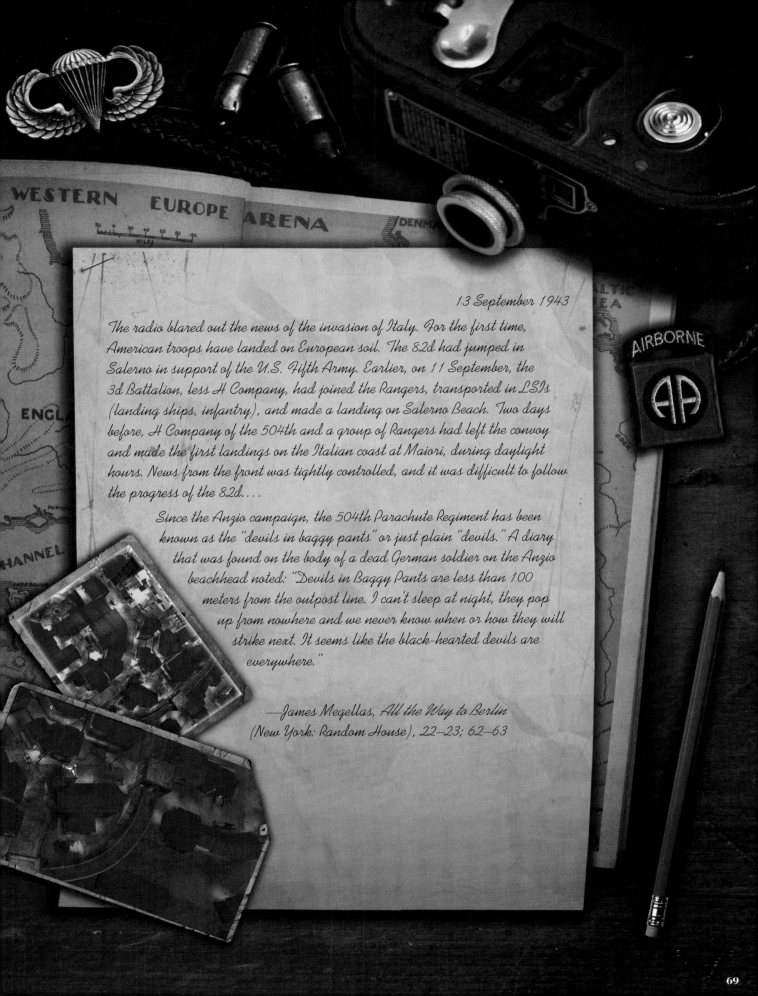

13 September 1943

The radio blared out the news of the invasion of Italy. For the first time, American troops have landed on European soil. The 82d had jumped in Salerno in support of the U.S. Fifth Army. Earlier, on 11 September, the 3d Battalion, less H Company, had joined the Rangers, transported in LSIs (landing ships, infantry), and made a landing on Salerno Beach. Two days before, H Company of the 504th and a group of Rangers had left the convoy and made the first landings on the Italian coast at Maiori, during daylight hours. News from the front was tightly controlled, and it was difficult to follow the progress of the 82d. . . .

Since the Anzio campaign, the 504th Parachute Regiment has been known as the "devils in baggy pants" or just plain "devils." A diary that was found on the body of a dead German soldier on the Anzio beachhead noted: "Devils in Baggy Pants are less than 100 meters from the outpost line. I can't sleep at night, they pop up from nowhere and we never know when or how they will strike next. It seems like the black-hearted devils are everywhere."

—James Megellas, All the Way to Berlin
(New York: Random House), 22–23; 62–63

Briefing

The paratroopers were not supposed to support the invasion of Italy. However, General Clark's soldiers of the Fifth Army who made the landings at Salerno have come under constant counterattack, resulting in heavy losses. The Germans have set up staging areas near the coast to supply these attacks. The largest of these is located near the Paestum archeological project outside Salerno. The Germans are dug in and well protected among the ruins. We must dismantle their operations piece by piece.

LEGEND

Objectives

- Sabotage Fuel Containers
- Destroy Ammo Cache
- Disable Communications Radio
- Disable Communications Antenna
- Assemble with the Fifth Army Demo Team
- Defeat Enemy Ambush
- Assemble with Corporal Kish
- Ascend to Hilltop Temple
- Destroy AA Gun
- Set Signal Fires for P-40 Warhawks

Secure Zones
(inside light green overlay)

- Southwest of Amphitheatre
- Southeast of Amphitheatre

Skill Drops

- Land on top of the column
- Land through the open archway
- Land through the opening
- Land on top of the water tower
- Land on top of the cargo loader

Weapon Pickups

- M12 Shotgun
- M12 Shotgun
- Machine Gun Positions
- Health

Miscellaneous

- Ladder
- Gate

Weapon Loadout

- M1928 Thompson or MP40
- M1903 Springfield
- M1911 Colt .45

History

The British Eighth Army began the invasion of Italy by beginning to land troops at the tip of the toe of the peninsula on September 3rd under the codename Operation Baytown. Operation Avalanche was the American landings at Salerno on September 9th, 150 miles to the north of the British landings. On the previous day, the 82nd Airborne Division was in the air and on its way to drop on Rome. However, this operation was cancelled at the last minute when it was learned that the Germans had at least two divisions of troops already in the city and that the drop would be a suicide mission.

The landings at Salerno met heavy resistance. Even though Italy had surrendered on the 8th of September, a German division was waiting with five more able to move in within a matter of days. By the 12th, the Salerno beachhead was in doubt. General Mark Clark, Commander of the U.S. Fifth Army, disembarked from the ship that had been his headquarters, and hit the beaches. He personally rallied and gave orders to his troops, leading from the front during the major German counterattack that took place on the 13th. In order to get reinforcements where they were needed quickly, Clark ordered paratroopers from the 504th Regiment, 82nd Airborne to drop in on the night of the 13th. More paratroopers were dropped the following night. On the 16th, the Germans launched their last counterattack. The British and U.S. armies were able to link up the next day and by the 18th, the Allies began moving out of the beachhead and advancing northwest toward Naples and then Rome.

PAESTUM

SECURE THE PAESTUM RUINS

You will be dropping right into the middle of some ancient Roman ruins outside of Salerno. The Germans have set up a base here and you must cause as much damage as possible to prevent this base from being used to support the counterattacks on the Allied landings. To begin with, you must eliminate the German's communications abilities, sabotage their motor pool area, and destroy their cache of weapons. There are no Italian Blackshirts here because Italy has surrendered. Instead you will face German Heer infantry and officers, as well as the tougher Waffen SS infantry.

LANDING IN PAESTUM

This is another night drop. However, the area below is pretty well lit.

Your drop zone is the central part of the Paestum ruins. Two SZs have been established to the southwest and southeast of the amphitheatre. At each you can find weapons ammo as well as health and both are safe from the enemy. However, if you are daring and willing to take on the Germans on your own initially, you can push your landing to the edge of the drop zone and bypass some of the defenses. For example, you can actually land in the motor pool, which will put you into position to blow up the fuel tanks there.

There are three objective areas. Two—the motor pool and ammo cache—are to the northeast, while the third—the communications equipment—is in the northwest. It does not matter in which order you accomplish your initial objectives. However, it is a good idea to go after the two in the northeast consecutively so you don't have to walk back and forth across the area more than necessary. Though there are no rooftops that you can climb up onto like in Adanti, there are still heights that can be used for an advantage, such as the aqueduct that runs east to west. If you brought the Springfield sniper rifle, you can use these heights to clear out areas from a distance before you rush in to complete your objectives.

Try landing in the aqueducts to gain a height advantage over the enemies below—especially with your sniper rifle.

SKILL DROPS

There are five skill drop locations in Paestum. While a couple help you achieve your objectives, the rest are just tests of your ability as a paratrooper

The first skill drop requires you to land on a pillar located near the western SZ. There is not a lot of space to land on, so you have to aim carefully and stick it. Flare at the last moment to slow down your descent. You can not engage the enemy at the objectives from this point, but you can take fire from the Germans in the amphitheatre. Shot them to score some kill points toward a weapon award with your rifle if you want.

This is actually the toughest skill drop to hit. You have to land through the open archway on the aqueduct designated by the parachute. The key is to move into position south of the archway, flaring to slow your descent. Then, as you approach the archway, flare and move toward it so you float through the archway and land in the aqueduct. From this position, you can engage some enemy troops near the upper excavation, as well as near the ammo cache.

3

This skill drop is in the lower excavation. You must not only drop down into the excavation but also through the doorway at the bottom. Since this is near the DZ center, you don't have to move laterally too much. Center yourself over the opening and face east. Then, as you are just going through the opening, flare and push forward to go through the doorway. This can put you right in the middle of a fight, so be ready for it. This skill drop is not very advantageous for the objectives. However, from this point, you can advance toward the ammo cache—after you get out of the excavation.

5

This is another tough landing. The cargo loader is located in the amphitheatre. However, you must land on a small platform on top of the loader to get the skill drop. Flare to get over to the loader and then line up with the platform. Flare at the last to make any adjustments and stick to the platform. You immediately come under fire from Germans in the amphitheatre to your north, so get down from the loader and take cover. Then, either kill the enemy, or get out of the amphitheatre and head to your objectives.

4

This is a cool skill drop. You have to land on top of the water tower in the middle of the motor pool. Since it is at the edge of the drop zone, you have to aim for it quickly and then flare several times to slow you down so you can get to it. You have a bit more room for landing than on the pillar, so that part is not too difficult. This is actually one of the best places to drop since from the water tower you can throw grenades to take out both fuel tanks. However, you also have a lot of enemies gunning for you as well—so be ready to fight.

Tips from the Developer

Take out the enemy in the central area first and your allies that are fighting there will be free to join you elsewhere.

SABOTAGE THE FUEL CONTAINERS

Cache

Ammo Cache

Fuel

Motor Pool

Fuel

Gap In Wall

Lower Excavation

Go down this ramp leading into the lower excavation to acquire a shotgun.

LEGEND

 Machine Gun Positions   ✚ Health

Miscellaneous

 Ladder   ← Recommended Path

Weapon Pickups

M12 Shotgun

Weapon Loadout

- M1928 Thompson or MP40
- M1903 Springfield
- M1911 Colt .45

Tips from the Developer

Rather than fighting your way through the lower excavation, take up a position on the outside and to the west so you can fire down on the enemy below while they are busy engaging your allies.

Eliminate the machine gunner blocking your way to the east.

The fuel containers are located in the motor pool area in the northeast. In order to get to it, you must fight your way from the central square through the area north of the lower excavation. A machine gun guards the gate leading to this eastern part of the map. There are a few different ways of dealing with the machine gun: One is to shoot the gunner. If you have a sniper rifle, that is fairly easy. That allows your allies to rush in and help you. If you landed in the aqueduct, you can also use this height advantage to take out the machine gunner. Another option is to enter the lower excavation and fight your way through so you can come out to the south of the machine gun and on its flank. Finally, you can land behind the machine gun or off to one side and take out the gunner.

If you go through the lower excavation, this area can be like a maze. Pick up the M12 shotgun by the entrance because it will come in handy in this close-quarters fight. Swap out your submachine gun for it. Keep an eye on your compass so you can see where the Germans are as you advance. Stay low and behind cover as you advance. Make your way to the southern edge, where you can take a path up and out of the excavations. The exits are to the east.

TIP

If you don't land on the aqueducts, you can still get up on them. Look for crates you can jump up onto or even a knocked over pillar that serves as a ramp to the top.

Pass through this area to get to the eastern edge of the motor pool area.

By coming around from the side, you can hit the enemy from behind, where they have no cover.

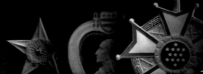 

When the pathway into the motor pool is open, you can move in. This area is defended pretty heavily. The Germans hide behind cover and even throw grenades at you. Upon entering the motor pool area, move east to the edge of the area, and then work your way north, taking out enemies as you go. You can try moving through the western or central parts of the motor pool, however the enemy are concentrated there and have lots of cover. You can often flank them from the east.

One of the fuel tanks is in the northern part of the motor pool. As soon as you see it and have cleared out the enemies near you, throw a grenade so it lands underneath the tank. When it detonates, it blows up the fuel tank. You can also fire at the fuel tank until it explodes.

The fuel tanks can take several shots before they explode—or you can use a grenade.

To save ammo, fire once at the fuel tank so it starts to leak. Then fire another shot at the puddle of fuel that collects.

Don't forget to get this western fuel tank as well.

The second fuel tank is in the western part of the motor pool. Continue advancing to the north and then make your way west along the northern edge. This helps keep Germans from hitting you from behind since you have the edge to your back. Watch out for enemies hiding in the tents or behind crates. When you get within range of

the second fuel tank, blow it up as well. Then all you have to do is mop up the remaining Germans and head for the next objective.

TIP

A sneaky way to destroy the fuel tanks is to infiltrate the motor pool from the northwest. If you go north from the eastern SZ, between the Amphitheatre and the motor pool, you find a gap in the wall leading into the motor pool. Once inside, you can move south along the wall to get to the western fuel tank to destroy it. Return to the gap and then move along the northern edge to get to the second fuel tank. You can then either fight your way through the motor pool, or head back through the gap.

DESTROY THE AMMO CACHE

The best way to get to the ammo cache is to parachute down into this area to the east of the lower excavations and as far south as possible. If you are already on the ground, come at it through the gate by the motor pool or by making your way through the lower excavations. Many enemies are in the courtyard. You must get past them and then enter the building area, which is actually built into a small hill, to get to the cache.

You must get past these enemies to get to the ammo cache.

TIP

If you need some health, a couple of these goodies can be found in the cave on the eastern side of the lower excavations.

The best way to advance to the building is to head south and then move up a rise in the earth. From behind stone walls, you can fire into the flanks of the German defenders, allowing your allies to push forward and help you clear out the rest. You can advance along this southern edge until it is time to enter the building. By this time, your allies should be helping with suppressing fire. Rather than going through the door in the center, jump through the window

Move along this southern pathway to flank the Germans.

When the outside of the building is clear, jump through this window.

to the south. Be ready to fire on Germans directly to the north who may be firing through windows at your allies.

Plant a charge here, and then run as fast as you can to get out before the roof comes crashing down!

TIP

One of the weapons dropped by the Germans is the G43 rifle. This is an excellent weapon in that it is a semiautomatic rifle that can be upgraded to include a scope and used as a sniper rifle. If you did not bring a Springfield sniper rifle with you, be sure to pick one up. Even if you did bring a Springfield, after using it for clearing out areas at a distance, pick up a G43 and start using it to earn weapon awards.

Germans lurk around most corners.

The subterranean building is like a maze of short walls and crates. Advance with caution and watch out for grenades thrown by the enemy. A shotgun or submachine gun works best in here. Make your way through the crates to the eastern edge of this building. It is important to clear as you go so you don't have to worry about enemies behind you. The Germans fire at you and then usually withdraw, so by the time you get to the end of the building where you set the charge, there may be a few Germans remaining. Throw a cooked grenade into their corner so they don't have time to run away. Finish off any survivors and then place the explosives on the crates where indicated. As soon as you do, sprint out of the building as fast as you can so the secondary explosions do not kill you as all the ammo goes up in flames.

DISABLE THE COMMUNICATIONS ANTENNA

LEGEND

Machine Gun Positions   **Health**

Miscellaneous

Ladder   ← Recommended Path

Gate

Weapon Pickups

2 M12 Shotgun

Weapon Loadout

- M1928 Thompson or MP40   • M1911 Colt .45
- M1903 Springfield

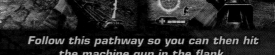

Follow this pathway so you can then hit the machine gun in the flank.

Both of the objectives dealing with communications are in the northwest. In order to get to the communications post, you will have to advance through the upper excavation and the restoration temple. The entrance to this area is covered by a machine gun. The best way to approach is from the direction of the western SZ. Follow a path to the west and take cover behind a stone wall. From this flank position, you can fire at the machine gunner. Stay here until all of the Germans around the machine gun have been eliminated and your allies are rushing forward toward the upper excavation.

This gate is locked from the other side. You must go through the upper excavation and restoration temple in order to get to the communications post.

Near the machine gun you find an M12 shotgun. If you have not already picked one up, grab this one. It makes the next part of the mission much easier because you will be fighting up close as you go through the ruins.

Watch for grenades as you clear out the excavation.

Head down the ramp into the excavation. Lots of Germans are in this area; be ready for them to throw grenades at you. With a shotgun, you don't have to worry about using ironsights as much when the enemy is up close. You can use grenades in the excavation, but be careful because you may hit your allies.

Climb up this ladder onto the wall and then continue to this second ladder to reach higher in the temple scaffolding.

When the bottom part of the excavation is clear, go up the wooden ramp. Rather than continuing on into the temple, take a right on the scaffolding and continue around to the ladder in the eastern part of the excavation. This takes you up to the top of a wall that you can walk across to some more scaffolding. Follow it to another ladder at the edge of the temple and climb up to begin going through the restoration temple on the second level of scaffolding.

Germans are not only in the center of the scaffolding, but also around the perimeter.

This ladder leads to the top level.

The temple has more Germans and they are careful to hide behind cover, popping up to fire at you or throw grenades. Take cover behind some crates at the southern end of the temple on this level and begin killing enemies as they show themselves. Some are near the temple's center and others are near the western and northern edges. After you have cleared out some of these, advance to the left along the scaffolding and then up the ramp to the next level. Continue to where the central enemies were to find a ladder. This quickly takes you to the top level. Watch out for Germans directly to the north when you get to the top. Throw a grenade or get rid of them with your shotgun before they can hurt you.

Jump across to this pillar and then onto the opposite walkway.

By this time, the temple area should be clear. Follow the scaffolding back to the west, picking up some health where those Germans on the top level were if you need it. Locate the top of a pillar. Jump over onto the pillar and then jump

Whack this console to destroy the antenna.

again to the scaffolding on the opposite side. You can also climb up onto the top western edge of the temple by jumping up on some crates in the southwest corner and then moving north to the scaffolding. Follow this walkway north and around a corner to locate the controls for the communications antennae. Hit it with a melee attack to destroy it and complete an objective.

Use your rifle to clear out the area below of Germans.

Several Germans are down at the communications post below you and to the north. Use your rifle to pick off as many as possible—especially those soldiers manning the machine gun. When it is clear, climb down the nearby ladder and proceed over to the gate. Shoot the lock and the gate opens, allowing allies to come directly to your position rather than having to advance through the excavation and temple.

Rather than climbing down to shoot the lock, if you have the Springfield or G43, you can shoot the lock from the top of the scaffolding. This lets your allies in while you stay up high to support them with rifle fire.

Toss a grenade into the tent to clear out the Germans inside—and some of the radio equipment.

Take cover behind some crates and engage the Germans as they appear out of the tents to the north. Advance along the eastern side of the communications post. The radio you must destroy is in the northwestern tent. Using crates for cover, head north, and watch for Germans. Move to a position from where you can throw a grenade into the tent containing the radio. Usually a few Germans are inside, so cook the grenade before you throw it. Once it goes off, move in to finish off any survivors. If not all of the parts of the radio are destroyed, use a melee attack to complete the job and save ammo. The enemy communications have now been destroyed and another objective is completed.

Move in to finish off anything that survived the grenade.

Assemble with the Fifth Army Demo Team

Now that you have secured the Paestum ruins, elements of the Fifth Army have arrived to help you eliminate the German presence in this area.

The Germans have a position on the hilltop temple. However, in order to get to them, you must blow up a massive steel gate. Fifth Army has send a demolitions team to do this for you. They are at the amphitheatre, so advance there to meet them. You should not run into any enemies on the way because you cleared out the ruins already. However, if you did not take time to mop up the Germans in the central area, do so now. Then the allies engaging them join up with you to move to the amphitheatre.

Time to enter the amphitheatre.

If you need ammo or health, stop by one of the SZs and resupply for the next part of the mission.

DEFEAT THE ENEMY AMBUSH

German infantry ambush you at the amphitheatre.

Return fire from behind cover, then run for an alcove.

Clear out the Germans around the amphitheatre.

ASSEMBLE WITH CORPORAL KISH

Head to the central square to receive new orders.

Upon arriving at the amphitheatre, you are attacked by Germans. These are Waffen SS infantry, which are tougher than the Heer infantry you have been facing so far. The enemy take up positions above you on the perimeter of the amphitheatre. While you can find some cover and start returning fire, be careful because they are all around and cover in one direction may not protect you from enemies behind you. Instead, run toward one of the alcoves at the edges of the amphitheatre and then carefully ascend the stairs to the upper level. Use your rifle to take out the Germans one by one. If you need health, go back down the stairs. Most of the alcoves contain health for you to pick up. Finish off all of the enemies, watching your compass to see where remaining foes may be hiding. After they have been eliminated, you get new orders.

After surviving the ambush, the demolitions team is now ready to open the way to the hilltop temple. Exit the amphitheatre, stopping to gather ammo or health as needed, and then move out toward the central square. The Fifth Army soldiers place charges on the steel door and then help you with your next objectives.

DESTROY THE AA GUN

The Germans have positioned artillery on the hilltop next to the temple that are being used to shell the U.S. troops at the Salerno beachhead. Your new orders are to get up to the temple, destroy the AA gun there, and then set signal fires so an airstrike can take out the position.

Lower Hilltop Temple

Hilltop Entrance

Barrel

Hilltop Temple

Barrel

Antiair Gun

NOTE

If you have been using your G43 regularly, you may have been able to earn the first two upgrades—a larger magazine and a sniper scope. This turns the German rifle into a semiautomatic sniper rifle that can fire 20 rounds before it has to reload!

Cross to the western side so you can come up behind this German at a machine gun.

As it begins to clear, move south a bit and take cover behind another wall so you can clear out the area to the west of you. When the enemy is gone and your allies have moved up, rush across to the western side of this area. Now go up the stairs, staying as far west as you can, then up another flight to come in behind a machine gun. Kill the soldier manning the machine gun and clear out this area. Then you can either man the gun yourself, or wait for one of your allies to take it over.

LEGEND

🔫 Machine Gun Positions   ➕ Health

Miscellaneous

◄— Recommended Path

Weapon Loadout

- M1928 Thompson or MP40
- M1903 Springfield
- M1911 Colt .45

ASCEND TO THE HILLTOP TEMPLE

Pick off enemies from a distance with your rifle if you can.

The doorway to the hilltop temple has been opened. However, a lot of Germans stand between you and your objectives. As soon as you step through the opened gate, you come under enemy fire. Head to the downed pillar on the left and take cover behind it. Try to pick off some of the Germans behind the walls to the south if you can. However, don't stay there long. Follow the dirt path to your left up the side of the hill and take cover behind the wall on the right when you

Take this path along the right side so you can reach the German flank.

get to the top. From here, begin to kill the Germans who are firing down on your allies below. Move around the corner carefully and hit them in the flanks. Be ready for the enemy to come after you and try to drive you away. Stay behind cover and pop up or around the cover for quick shots.

Shoot at the Germans to the east.

You are now fighting against enemies to the east. Pick off as many as you can with your rifle or shotgun from this location, then begin advancing east. Rush from cover to cover, and stay north as you continue moving east, watching for enemies hiding or throwing grenades at you. When you get to the eastern end, ascend the stairs to the southeast, using the same tactics as before. When you reach the steps at the southern end of the walkway that lead up to the temple, pause for your allies to catch up and make sure your weapons are fully loaded.

TIP

Getting to the hilltop can be deadly. The best tactic is to stay back and pick off Germans at the top of the stairs from a distance using your rifle. If you have a sniper rifle, this is a lot easier because you can stay back from the gate to do this. As you clear out an area, your fellow paratroopers advance to secure it. Then move forward to clear the next area.

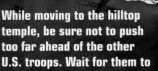
While moving to the hilltop temple, be sure not to push too far ahead of the other U.S. troops. Wait for them to catch up, or even lead as you advance to the top. Listen to what they say. If you hear one ask you to cover them, start laying down suppressive fire on the enemy while your ally rushes forward to take them out. If you don't help, your ally usually gets killed.

Head through the interior of the temple.

There is a machine gun to the west of the stairs, covering this way up to the temple area. Make sure you are crouched down and carefully climb the stairs, keeping your right shoulder next to the wall. At the top is a short stone that you can hide behind. Peek around it to the left and use your rifle to kill the gunner up ahead. Wait for your allies to move past you, then advance and turn to the right. Hide behind some crates and then pop up to use your rifle to take out the soldier manning another machine gun to the north. You can also use grenades.

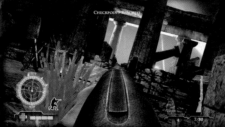

Ascend these steps and then take out the soldier at the machine gun.

Now move through the temple's interior, clearing any remaining enemies inside, and take cover behind some stone walls or crates in the southwestern part of temple so you can neutralize the enemies around the AA gun. Advance

From this position, use your rifle to clear the area around the AA gun.

from cover to cover as you get clear the area. Your allies help you and even rush forward to flush out your foes. Throw a grenade or two to get those enemies who are hiding behind sandbags and be ready to shoot them if they try to run for it. When it is clear, move forward and place a charge on the AA gun to destroy it and complete another objective.

Eliminate the Germans near the artillery and prevent them from getting to the machine gun.

Advance carefully toward the machine gun you just cleared, eliminating any Germans who move in to take control of it. Continue to the crates to the west of the machine gun and take cover behind them. From this spot, pick off several enemies that come at you from the west. Keep this up until they are all eliminated.

Blow up this AA gun.

SET SIGNAL FIRES FOR P-40 WARHAWKS

Shoot two of the red barrels to start signal fires.

All that remains to do is set some signal fires so that American P-40s can make their bombing run on the artillery guns. Head north from the AA gun toward the area in front of the temple. Two red barrels are in this area. Shoot each a couple of times to set them ablaze and complete your final objective for the mission.

The P-40s zoom in and destroy the artillery to prevent it from ever again firing on Allied troops at Salerno.

OPERATION NEPTUNE

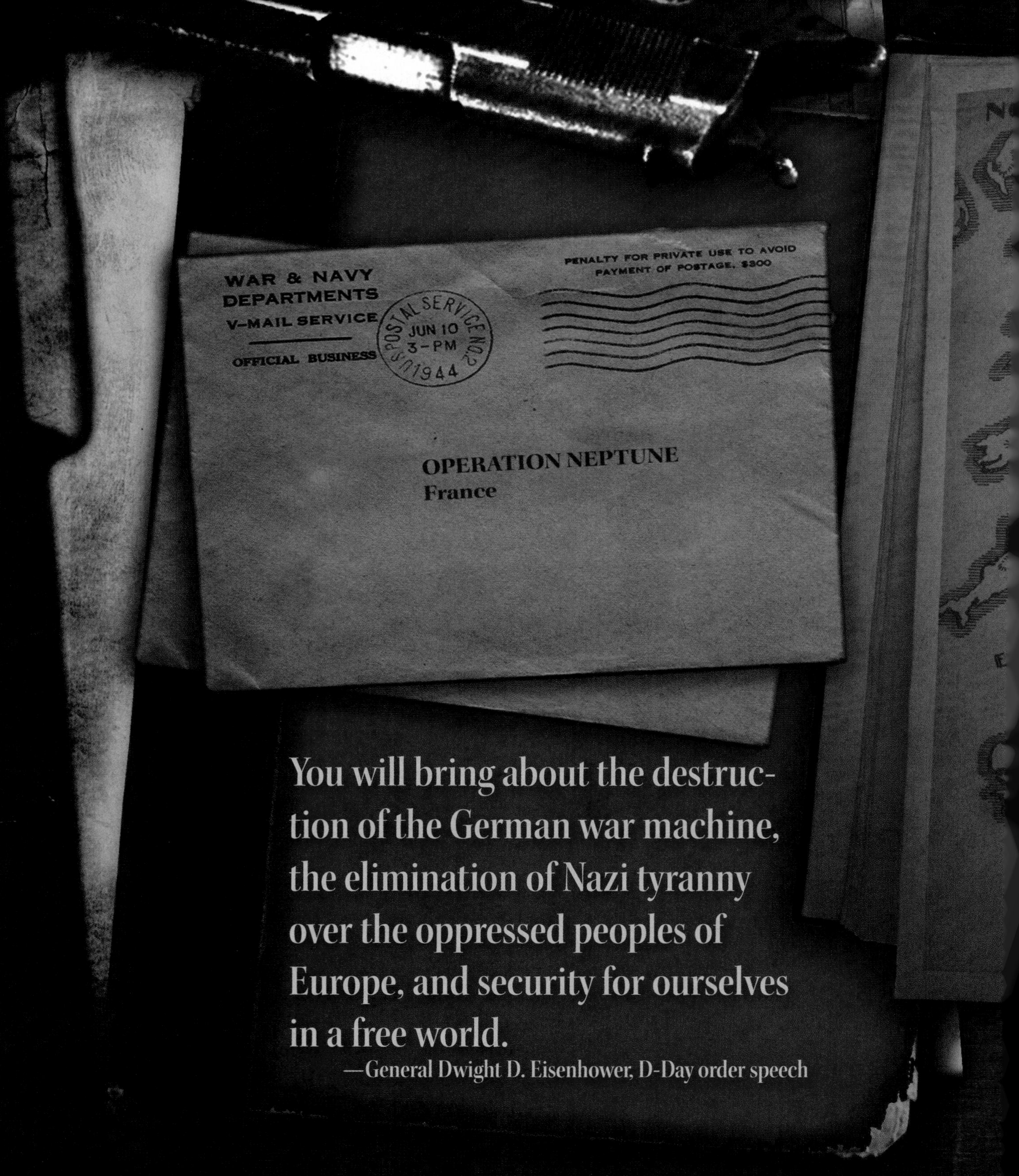

WAR & NAVY
DEPARTMENTS
V–MAIL SERVICE
_____
OFFICIAL BUSINESS

US POSTAL SERVICE NO. 2
JUN 10
3 – PM
1944

PENALTY FOR PRIVATE USE TO AVOID
PAYMENT OF POSTAGE, $300

OPERATION NEPTUNE
France

You will bring about the destruction of the German war machine, the elimination of Nazi tyranny over the oppressed peoples of Europe, and security for ourselves in a free world.

—General Dwight D. Eisenhower, D-Day order speech

05 June 1944

On the night of 5 June 1944, the pathfinder aircraft, of the IX Troop Carrier Command, took off from Witham airfield, and shortly thereafter troop carriers carrying the three parachute regiments took off from airfields scattered around England. The pathfinders from the 504th Parachute Regiment were the first to land on French soil. After ten days on the ground, they were relieved and returned to the regiment, but not before seven troopers from the 504th were killed. The long-awaited invasion of Hitler's European fortress was under way. I remember standing in the company street on the memorable night of 5 June and seeing the sky full of C-47s flying over Leicester. I had an empty feeling in my stomach as I watched those planes heading for France without me. I felt like a bride left at the altar.

On 8 July, the 82d Airborne returned to England after 33 days of combat without relief or replacements. During that time, the four regiments of the 82d successfully completed every assigned mission. Paratroopers of the 505th liberated Ste. Mere Eglise, the first city to be taken from the Germans in France, four hours before the beach landing on D-Day.... During the fighting, the 82d had destroyed 62 German tanks and 44 antitank and artillery guns, while sustaining 46 percent casualties.

—James Megellas, *All the Way to Berlin*
(New York: Random House), 105–106

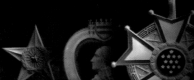

MEDAL OF HONOR
AIRBORNE

During the early hours of D-Day, you are dropped inland from the coast of Normandy in order to support the Allied landings at Utah Beach. The Germans have built a veritable fortress to repel an invasion force. Your mission is to eliminate their ability to fire on Allied ships so that the naval warships can close to fire shore bombardment and the landing craft can make it safely to the beaches to unload their cargo of soldiers.

LEGEND

Objectives

- **Collect M18 Bundles (4)**
- **Knock Out Tiger Tank**
- **Clear and Secure Spotting Tower**
- **Destroy Radar Antenna Relay**
- **Clear Central Casemate**
- **Clear and Secure Pillboxes (2)**

Secure Zones
(inside light green overlay)

- **In the south near the cottage**

Skill Drops

- **Land on top of the cement wall**
- **Land on the small rooftop**
- **Land in the room on the second floor**
- **Land through the pillbox door**
- **Land inside the destroyed house**

Weapon Pickups

- **M1928 Thompson submachine gun**
- **M1 Garand rifle**
- **Machine Gun Positions**
- **Health**

Miscellaneous

- **Ladder**
- **Gate**

Weapon Loadout

- **M1928 Thompson or M12 Shotgun**
- **M1903 Springfield or G43**
- **M1911 Colt .45**

AUDOUVILLE

History

Operation Neptune was the name given to the assault phase of the D-Day invasion known as Operation Overlord. The Airborne played an important role in Neptune. Over 13,000 paratroopers from the the 82nd and 101st Airborne Divisions loaded aboard 822 transport planes and were dropped into Normandy before sunrise on 6 June 1944. Their main objective was to prevent German reinforcements from getting to the beaches for a counterattack against the landings. In order to do this, the paratroopers were to block the approaches to the beaches as well as secure the exits from the beaches and capture key bridges so that the Allied infantry from Utah beach could advance toward its objectives.

The 82nd's 505th regiment landed the most accurately of all the regiments, with over half of the paratroopers landing within one mile of their drop zones and three-quarters within two miles. The 508th, on the other hand, dropped only a quarter of its paratroopers within a mile of their drop zone. Nearly half of the regiment landed on the wrong side of the Merderet river and were unable to complete their mission.

Of the missions assigned to the 82nd Airborne, only one was completed according to plan—the capture of Sainte-Mère-Église. The 3rd Battalion of the 505th was able to assemble fairly quickly and moved into the town. So that enemy fire could be detected in the darkness, the paratroopers were ordered to use only bayonets, knives, and grenades. The Germans had only about 40 soldiers in the town and about 30 of them were captured as the town was taken by the Americans before dawn.

Those paratroopers who were not lucky enough to drop close enough to their units or their objectives still did what they could to disrupt the German response to the invasion. As a result, it took a while for the German command to know exactly where the main airborne body was in order to respond. By the end of the day on 6 June, the 82nd had lost 165 men killed in action.

SECURE THE AUDOUEVILLE BATTERY

The German coastal guns are a serious threat to the Allied invasion fleet and must be put out of action. In order to accomplish that, you first must secure your SZ against enemy counterattack by armored units. To help shut down the guns so Allied warships can sail in closer to bombard the defenses, you will need to secure a spotting tower whose calls help direct artillery fire and neutralize the enemy's radar capability.

The terrain here in Normandy is different than you experienced in Sicily or Italy. You will be advancing uphill as you move north. Trees and hedges cut the area into narrow paths. The open areas are filled with trench lines that cut into the ground. These trenches are filled with Germans who want to kill you. There are also several machine gun positions that cover most of the main approaches to your objectives, so you must deal with them.

The enemy you face here are more experienced. To the south, you will mostly face Heer infantry. However, as you advance north to the more important objectives, you will engage Waffen SS infantry and Waffen SS officers. These troops are tough, taking more damage and moving around much more to kill you. Therefore, use caution during a firefight and be sure to pick up ammo as you find it—you don't want to run out in the middle of an engagement and have to rely on your pistol.

LANDING IN AUDOUEVILLE

Your plane comes under heavier fire than before. As you drop, you can see the area below. Your SZ is in the south.

Unlike the previous two missions, this one is a day drop. Therefore, you can see the area below as you drop much better. The drop zone consists of most of the southern portion of the map. The SZ is adjacent to a cottage where you can pick up ammo, health, and a few weapons. From here, you can go after any of your initial objectives.

One of your objectives is to gather the four M18 bundles. This will let you use the M18 recoilless rifle, which you will need to destroy a German Tiger tank—another of your objectives. The other two objectives are located to the north. On the western side of the map is the large radar array. You must put it out of action. To the east of the radar is a spotting tower. This objective requires you to clear out the tower to prevent it from being used to call in artillery strikes against the Allied landings on Utah beach.

The cottage near the SZ is stocked with lots of ammo, weapons, and health. Think of it as your base and a good place to land.

SKILL DROPS

There are five skill drop locations in Audoueville. Each of them provides some type of tactical advantage you can use to help your allies advance toward an objective or puts you in a position from which you can work to complete an objective on your own.

This first skill drop is on the spotting tower. You must land on a wall, which does not give you much space to stick a landing. In addition, this location is at the drop zone's edge, so to get to it, flare and move toward it when you jump out of the plane. This spot also gives you a great position to take out the machine gunner guarding the entrance to the spotting tower. However, don't stay up on the wall for long, or the Germans in the trenches below will take you down.

This skill drop is on the destroyed barn at the map's southern end. To complete this drop, land on the small portion of the higher rooftop remaining. It is not too far from where you drop, so you only need to flare a bit to get over this location. From here, you can pick up the M18 bundle on the roof and start working on that objective. Just be ready for the Tiger tank that arrives as soon as you pick up the first bundle.

3 This skill drop is in the cottage. You must land inside the second floor room where the roof and one wall have been blown away by combat. This is actually a great place to land. Quickly take cover behind the chest of drawers and begin picking off Germans to the north with your rifle. This allows your allies to advance to the destroyed house to the north.

4 This skill drop is the most difficult for this mission. You must land through the door of a pillbox located to the south of the spotting tower. To do this, you must flare a lot and move past the pillbox, then turn to face the door, flaring at the last minute to move through the doorway. Be ready for an enemy inside. By eliminating this threat and then clearing away the nearby trenches, you can clear the way for your allies to advance up the eastern side of the map toward the spotting tower.

5 The final skill drop is inside the destroyed house north of the cottage. You must land in the room filled with rubble, making this a tough place to get a good landing. Usually a German is in the next room, so be ready to fight as soon as you can pull up your gun. From here, begin your advance on either the radar bunker or the spotting tower.

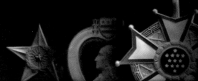

COLLECT M18 BUNDLES

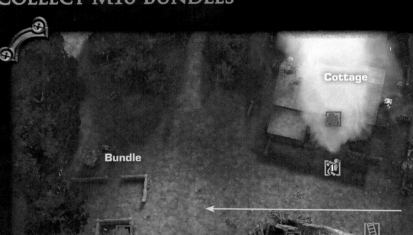

Cottage

Bundle

Bundle

Bundle

Destroyed Barn

Tiger Tank

Bundle

LEGEND

 Machine Gun Positions   Health

Secure Zones
(inside light green overlay)

In the south near the cottage

Miscellaneous

Ladder   ← Recommended Path

Weapon Loadout

- M1928 Thompson or M12 Shotgun
- M1903 Springfield or G43
- M1911 Colt .45

Since the bundle on the roof is the toughest to get with a tank around, start with it. If you didn't land on the roof, take this ladder up to the top.

This is usually a good objective with which to begin the mission. However, you also can do it after completing the other two initial objectives. All you have to do is move to four bundles and pick up the pieces of the M18 recoilless rifle. However, as soon as you pick up one bundle, a German Tiger tank arrives on the scene and begins to attack. Therefore, it is usually a good idea to start with the bundle on the top of the destroyed barn. When you drop, land on the roof of the barn or even try for the skill drop location on the small section of roof that is higher than the rest. After landing, pick up the part from the bundle and get ready to move.

The Tiger tank arrives. Get off the roof!

The Tiger tank appears from the east. It is armed with two different weapons. Its 88mm main gun can kill you with a direct hit. However, you can still take blast damage from a near miss as well. The tank is also armed with a bow machine gun that can only fire in the tank's front arc. Try to stay to the side or rear of the tank so you only have to worry about its main gun. The other three bundles are located to the north, west, and south of the destroyed barn. The key to reaching all the bundles is to use the barn as cover. Move west along the roof and hop down into the second-floor room of the barn to get some cover from the tank. It usually begins to roll forward toward the west. As it approaches the barn, get down to the ground and go for the southern bundle. Pick up the part and then return to the barn so that it is between you and the tank.

TIP

It takes some time for the main gun to reload, so wait for it to fire before rushing to the next bundle. As you approach, find some cover and wait for the next shot. Then pick up the M18 part and find cover again.

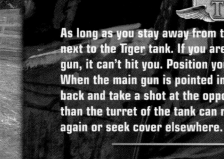

Quickly pick up the remaining three bundles.

Depending on where the tank is, go after either the western or northern bundle. Each is near some stone walls behind which you can hide for cover. The western bundle is one of the toughest because you must traverse a lot of open ground to get to it. However, once you have picked up three bundles, at the location of the fourth, you trade in one of your weapons for the M18 recoilless rifle: Now you change from being the hunted to the hunter.

At the last bundle, you will be able to pick up the M18 recoilless rifle.

KNOCK OUT TIGER TANK

Aim for the treads or the side of the tank where the armor is weakest.

Use the barn for cover and keep hitting the tank on the same side.

TIP

As long as you stay away from the front, you can get right up next to the Tiger tank. If you are under the barrel of the main gun, it can't hit you. Position yourself on one side of the tank. When the main gun is pointed in your direction, run around the back and take a shot at the opposite side. You can move quicker than the turret of the tank can rotate. Then, either get up close again or seek cover elsewhere.

With the M18 in your hands, rush back to the barn to use it as cover. The Tiger usually follows you around, so find a spot and wait for the tank to come to you. The Tiger tank is heavily armored. It can take a lot of hits to its front and keep going. Therefore, go for its weak spots—the sides and treads. Your first shot should be aimed at the tread wheels on one side of the tank. After firing, get back behind cover while you reload and the tank's main gun fires. Then move out to hit the tank in the tread on the same side as before. A second hit causes the tank to throw a track, effectively immobilizing it. Now just get a third hit on the same side and the tank should be history.

Three hits to a side knock out the Tiger tank. It takes more hits if you are aiming at the front.

TIP

If you need more ammo for the recoilless rifle, look for a crate in the southeast corner of the barn and another crate in front of the cottage. After taking out the tank, use the M18 against some infantry and earn some kill points so you can upgrade it for future use. Just be sure to aim at the ground or a wall behind them so the blast damage kills them as well as nearby enemies.

CLEAR AND SECURE THE SPOTTING TOWER

The spotting tower is in the eastern part of the map. This can be a tough place to get to from the southern part of the map where the SZ is located. You must fight your way through trenches and risk fire from three different machine guns guarding this route. However, if you take your time and work with your allies, it is not too difficult. The best weapons for this part of the mission are a shotgun or submachine gun and a rifle because you want to be able to take out as many Germans at long range as possible, but also need some heavy firepower for close up fights.

Rush up to this stone wall and take cover. From here you can take out the gunner in the pillbox.

There are two main routes to get to the spotting tower. The eastern route takes you up the hill right under the sights of the machine guns as you maneuver to outflank them. Start off near the red truck and then take the path to the right. Stay to the right at the next branch and then, when you get to a stone wall on your left, sprint forward to a corner in another stone wall that provides cover from the north as well as the east. A pillbox up ahead contains a machine gun that the Germans use to fire down on you along this trail. From this spot by the stone wall, you can use your rifle to take out the gunner.

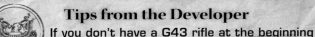

Tips from the Developer

If you don't have a **G43** rifle at the beginning of this mission, be sure to pick one up as soon as you can find one dropped by an enemy soldier. Not only does the German weapon hold ten rounds to the M1 Garand's eight, but you can also reload it in the middle of a clip; with the Garand, you have to fire all eight rounds before reloading.

EASTERN ROUTE

Follow the path by the red truck.

TIP

If you have a sniper rifle, stand on the crate by the red truck and you can get a shot at the gunner inside the pillbox.

Spotting
Tower

Parking

Middle

Western
Route

Cottage

Eastern
Route

*Clear out the
trenches as you
advance.*

LEGEND

Machine Gun Positions   Health

Miscellaneous

Ladder   ←——— Recommended Path

Gate

Weapon Loadout

- M1928 Thompson or M12
  Shotgun

- M1903 Springfield or G43

- M1911 Colt .45

This concrete walkway leads up to the Spotting Tower entrance from the eastern direction.

Clearing out the pillbox allows your allies to join up with you. Your next threats are soldiers to the east. They come along the trench line, taking cover behind crates and walls. Clear and advance to the eastern edge, then begin pushing north. While you can just go for the spotting tower, it is a good idea first to clear out the trenches. This allows allied replacements to get to you easier. Be sure to clear out each of the machine gun emplacements as well.

Tips from the Developer

The shotgun is a great weapon in the trenches as well as the bunker interiors.

WESTERN ROUTE

The western route begins at the cottage. Since you will be advancing through the destroyed house in the middle of the map, it is a good idea to clear it out first. Take up a position on the second floor of the cottage and use a rifle to snipe at

From the second floor of the cottage, you have a good vantage for sniping at the Germans in the destroyed house in the center of the map.

all the Germans around the destroyed house. The chest of drawers in the damaged room is a good spot for this. As you kill them one by one, your fellow paratroopers can advance up the tail leading to the destroyed house. As it clears out, return to the ground level and move up the trail yourself, mopping up any remaining enemies. Enter the destroyed house and move to the eastern room that is filled with rubble.

TIP

You can find crates of ammo, grenades, and health in the cottage, as well as an M1 Garand and a Thompson submachine gun. Consider the cottage your base for this mission since it is the only SZ on the map.

Crouch down and cautiously move to take cover behind the stone wall, to the left of what used to be a window. Peek to the right around this wall and engage any Germans in the trenches to the east of your position. When the trenches are clear, use your rifle to shoot the soldier on the machine gun uphill from the trench. Now that it's clear, go east. Barbed wire and dragon's teeth block the road leading up the hill, so you must go through the trenches. Stay

Take cover on the left side of this former window.

Watch for enemies to rush out as you advance.

along the trench's left side. As you get to the end of the wooden wall, hold. Another machine gun is up ahead to the left. Peek around the side or over the top to kill the gunner using your rifle. Or, throw a grenade into his position.

The parking area has several enemies in it. Throw a grenade to get some, then rush in to finish them off.

Continue moving uphill to the east until you come to an intersection. You can clear out the pillbox to the right if you want. Then move to the left toward the parking area. A well-placed grenade can take out several Germans in this area. Along with your allies, clear this area and then get ready to enter the spotting tower.

ASSAULT ON THE TOWER

The ground entrance is protected by this machine gun position.

Naval bombardment has blasted another entrance into the spotting tower. This is a safer way to enter. Clear out the enemies on this second level, then go up or down from there.

Climb up on the wall and shoot down through the firing port.

There are two ways into the spotting tower. The ground entrance on the western side is accessible by a concrete walkway from the east or a concrete side area filled with crates from the parking area. The problem with this entrance is that it is guarded by a machine gun at the end of a narrow corridor. To go in this way, you must kill the gunner with a rifle shot. If you climb up on the wall to the side, you can shoot down at the gunner and usually avoid being hit by his fire. When the way is clear, move into the tower before another German can man the machine gun.

Inside, move to the doorway and peek around the corner. There are several Germans in this bunkroom. Throw a grenade inside to kill some and get the rest to move so you can shoot them. Off to the right is a restroom and a stairway. Clear out these areas and then climb the stairs to the next level.

At the top of the stairs you find the second level has a gaping hole in the wall of the main room. Clear out the area near the stairs, and then move into the main room. The gaping hole is the second entrance into the tower and allows you to bypass the machine gun at the lower entrance. However, if you choose to come in through this way, you still need to clear the lower level to complete this objective.

Peek around the corner at the top of the stairs to engage the Germans in the tower's third level.

Now ascend the stairs to the third level. The room at the top contains the equipment used to determine the range for the German coastal artillery as they fired on Allied ships. Eliminate any enemies in this room, then go up the last flight of stairs to the top of the tower to completely secure the spotting tower. One more objective is now achieved.

This spotting device will not be used to target Allied ships anymore.

The combat inside the spotting tower is close and deadly.

TIP

While climbing the stairs, be sure to peek around every corner, ready to shoot any enemies waiting to ambush you.

Tips from the Developer

The spotting tower is not a bad choice for a first objective. In fact, if you feel like you can manage on your own, drop onto the skill drop on the concrete wall to begin the mission. Clear it out and then make your way to the top. From here, you can use a sniper rifle to take out Germans in the trenches below or rain down grenades on them.

DESTROY THE RADAR ANTENNA RELAY

Radar Relay

Middle

West Road

Cottage

LEGEND

Machine Gun Positions

Health

Miscellaneous

Ladder

← Recommended Path

Weapon Loadout

- M1928 Thompson or M12 Shotgun

- M1903 Springfield or G43

- M1911 Colt .45

Approach the area of the radar bunker from the east so that you are not a target for the pillbox.

Take out enemies protecting the bunker, especially the soldier on the machine gun.

The radar bunker is located in the west. Machine gun emplacements as well as trenches protect it. However, these defenses are not as large or elaborate as those south of the spotting tower. While the west road takes you right into the action, it is safer to advance on the radar bunker from the southeast. The area around the destroyed house in the middle must be cleared first. After that has been accomplished, continue along the path toward the radar defenses, taking cover behind the first stone wall you come to. From this spot, you can't be hit by the machine gun in the pillbox. However, you can hit the soldier manning the machine gun right in front of the bunker. Shoot him first using your rifle, and then take out as many other Germans as you can see from this position.

Move into the trenches and clear them of enemies.

As this area begins to clear, advance to the next stone wall along the eastern side of this area and shoot at more Germans. When you have killed as many as you can from here, switch to your shotgun or submachine gun and move west through the trenches toward the pillbox. This is a close fight as you come upon enemies behind crates and around corners down in the trenches. Work to secure the pillbox, and then head north toward the bunker. Keep an eye on the machine gun and kill any German who steps up to use it. Germans come out of the bunker on the eastern side, so advance to the concrete walkway, use one of the walls for cover, and peek around it to drop the enemies as they come at you.

When no more Germans emerge, advance along the walkway to the east. The bunker entrance is protected by another machine gun. However, if you come from the west and move just far enough so that you can see the opening through which the gun fires, you can throw a grenade inside and blow up the gunner. Be sure to cook the grenade for about four seconds so it explodes just as it is going through the opening. Before another German can man the gun, quickly go up the stairs and enter the bunker. A passageway leads to a control room where several enemies are usually holed up. Lob in some grenades, carefully bouncing them off the left wall so they go toward the enemies on the right. The grenades usually either kill the enemies near the doorway or force them to move back, allowing you to approach and peek around the doorway to fire at the remaining enemies inside.

Throw a grenade through this firing port to kill the gunner.

Then, as you enter, shoot through this second firing port to clear the room on the other side.

Clear the room to the north before going for the eastern rooms.

Enter the control room and move to take a position behind the counter so you are on the side opposite the doorway. Use your compass to locate more enemies. First, clear the room to the north, and then concentrate on the two rooms to the east. Use grenades to clear these rooms or at least flush the enemy out. Keep up the pressure until the entire bunker is clear.

This ladder leads to the roof.

Throw a grenade to the side of a support to get the German on the other side.

The room in the northeast contains a ladder; climb it to get up to the roof of the bunker where the radar relay is. Climb up and then crouch down as you exit the small shack on top. More enemies are on top of the bunker. Two are usually located behind supports to the west or south, and another is near the relay to the north of the support where you are positioned. Deal with the eastern two first. Throw a grenade so it lands between the two supports and you may be able to take out both enemies. Then maneuver around so you can peek past the corner to get a shot at the last enemy on the roof. When it is clear, move to the relay and set a charge to blow up the German's radar relay. Now that you have completed this objective is completed, descend the stairs on the eastern side and then jump over the crates.

Plant a charge on this relay to shut down the German radar.

NOTE

Now that you have completed all the initial objectives, a door near the radar bunker and a gate near the parking area open, allowing you to advance to the central casemate.

CLEAR THE CENTRAL CASEMATE

The trench area has lots of Germans. Kill them all.

Watch out for this machine gun next to the entrance.

You have received new orders—advance to the central casemate and clear it out. To get there, you must move through a small trench area to the south of the casemate. Depending on where you are when the initial objectives are completed, you can enter the trench area from either the east or the west—it doesn't really matter. Clear out the enemies from this area before approaching the casemate entrance. As with the other two structures, a machine gun guards the entrance. Either shoot the soldier behind the gun, or lob a grenade through the firing port to kill him.

Shoot through this firing port to clear the room.

Cautiously advance through the casemate, clearing out each room as you go.

At the entrance to the casemate, another firing port just past the doorway usually hides a soldier waiting to ambush you. Peek around the corner of the doorway and kill this soldier before entering. Then move up to the firing port and shoot through it to kill Germans in the room on the other side. Hold here while your allies move on into the room to help clear it, then follow them in. More enemies are in the next room to the left. Take up a position behind some crates and throw a grenade in to get the fight started. Slowly and cautiously advance to the doorway to shoot those hiding behind cover. Use the same tactics to clear the rest of the rooms inside the casemate to complete this objective.

CLEAR AND SECURE THE PILLBOXES

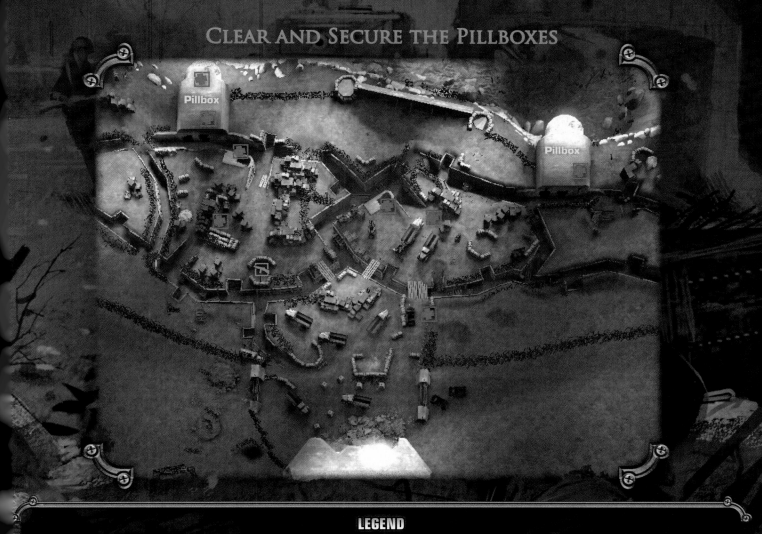

LEGEND

Miscellaneous

Machine Gun Positions   Health   ← Recommended Path

Weapon Loadout

- M1928 Thompson or M12 Shotgun   • M1911 Colt .45
- M1903 Springfield or G43

MEDAL OF HONOR
Airborne

The area out in front of the casemate is filled with crates, trucks, and trenches—as well as many Germans.

Support your allies by sniping at the enemies below—especially the machine gun position.

The final objective is to clear out the pillboxes overlooking the invasion beaches. Waffen SS officers are defending this area along with Waffen SS infantry. The officers are the toughest you have faced so far, so be ready. They can take a bit more damage, so be ready with an additional shot or burst, if necessary. When this part of the mission begins, quickly take cover behind concrete in the casemate. From this position, use your rifle to fire on enemies below. They will be firing back, so use caution. As you target and down these enemies, your allies can advance forward toward the pillboxes.

TIP

The Waffen SS officers are armed with the StG.44 automatic rifles. When you get a chance, but sure to pick one up. For greater accuracy, fire them in short bursts.

Make your way toward one of the pillboxes.

It does not matter which pillbox you go for first. As your troops begin to move forward, leave your perch on the casemate and move down to where the action is. Switch to your shotgun or submachine gun as you advance. Try to stay to one side of the area, either east or west, to avoid the enemies in the middle for now. As you approach one of the pillboxes, watch the firing port near the entrance. Often a soldier is there waiting to shoot you. Take him out and then enter. Peek around corners to see what you face. The pillboxes consist of two levels. You are entering at the top level. You can usually find a few soldiers in here. Clear them out with gunfire or grenades, then go down the stairs. Watch for enemies on the stairwell as you descend. The lower level is similar to the upper. Use the same tactic to completely secure this pillbox.

Lob a grenade into this area to blow up a couple of enemies. Then move in to finish off any survivors.

The area between the pillboxes is a real firefight. These Germans are tough.

You now have to clear out the second pillbox. There is a trench running between the two pillboxes. However, debris blocks the trench, forcing you to move through the middle of the area. Stacks of crates and other objects are useful cover as you cautiously move through here. Expect a lot of enemies. Work with your allies to clear a path to the next pillbox. Your compass is invaluable in helping you detect enemies that might be hiding in trenches or behind crates. It is usually best to stay out of the trenches. Instead, cross over them on the planks of wood.

Secure the second pillbox just like you did the first.

After you reach the second pillbox, use the same tactics as before. Watch for the firing port. Clear the upper level. Go down the stairs. Clear the lower level. When the second pillbox is secure, the mission is complete. You do not need to mop up any surviving enemies in the trench area.

With the coastal guns and pillboxes no longer a threat to Allies landing on the beaches, the paratroopers move on to other tasks.

OPERATION MARKET GARDEN

WAR & NAVY
DEPARTMENTS
V-MAIL SERVICE

OFFICIAL BUSINESS

U.S. POSTAL SERVICE No. 2
JUN 10
3 — PM
1944

PENALTY FOR PRIVATE USE TO AVOID
PAYMENT OF POSTAGE. $300

OPERATION MARKET GARDEN
Holland

It looks very rough. If I get through
this one I will be very lucky.
—Brigadier General James M. Gavin, commander 82nd
Airborne, from his diary prior to Market Garden

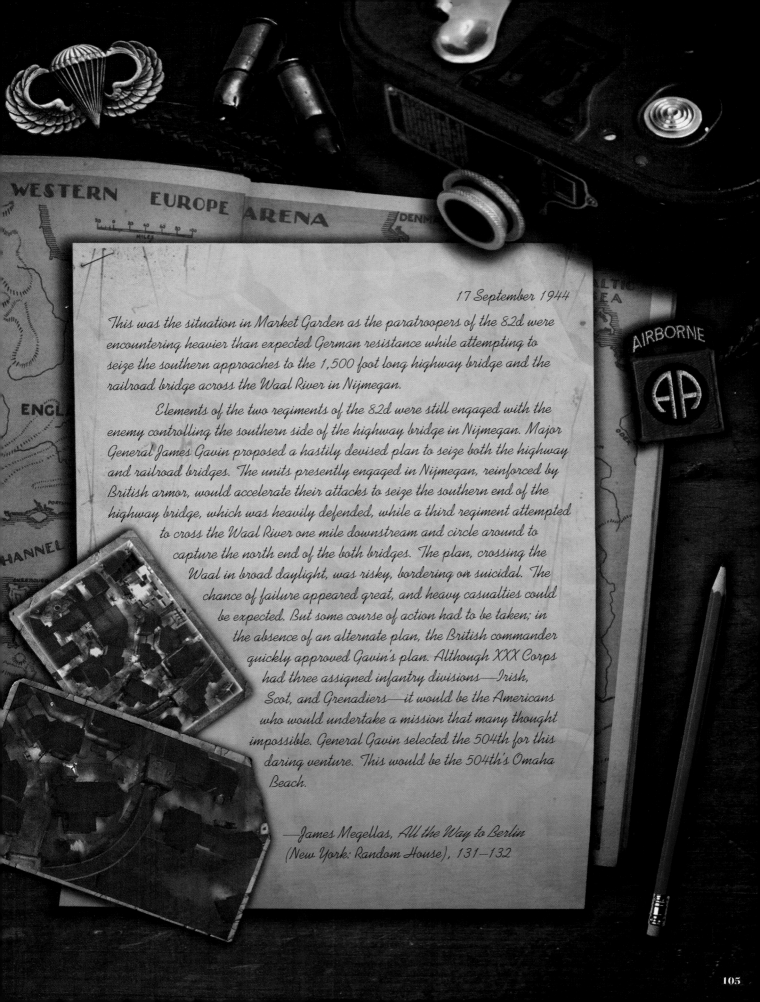

17 September 1944

This was the situation in Market Garden as the paratroopers of the 82d were encountering heavier than expected German resistance while attempting to seize the southern approaches to the 1,500 foot long highway bridge and the railroad bridge across the Waal River in Nijmegan.

Elements of the two regiments of the 82d were still engaged with the enemy controlling the southern side of the highway bridge in Nijmegan. Major General James Gavin proposed a hastily devised plan to seize both the highway and railroad bridges. The units presently engaged in Nijmegan, reinforced by British armor, would accelerate their attacks to seize the southern end of the highway bridge, which was heavily defended, while a third regiment attempted to cross the Waal River one mile downstream and circle around to capture the north end of the both bridges. The plan, crossing the Waal in broad daylight, was risky, bordering on suicidal. The chance of failure appeared great, and heavy casualties could be expected. But some course of action had to be taken; in the absence of an alternate plan, the British commander quickly approved Gavin's plan. Although XXX Corps had three assigned infantry divisions—Irish, Scot, and Grenadiers—it would be the Americans who would undertake a mission that many thought impossible. General Gavin selected the 504th for this daring venture. This would be the 504th's Omaha Beach.

—James Megellas, *All the Way to Berlin*
(New York: Random House), 131–132

MEDAL of HONOR
AIRBORNE

Briefing

Airborne, we are going for the knockout punch on this one. If we succeed we might be home by Christmas. Operation Market Garden requires airborne forces to secure several key bridges on the way to Arnhem. It is a risky plan. Our bridge is located in the town of Nijmegan. You must secure the town and take the bridge. The Germans would rather destroy the bridge than let it fall to us. We must find and disable any German explosives. Despite heavy Allied bombing, the enemy continues to operate heavy armored units. Eliminate any and all threats from this sector. You are dropping into territory that is firmly in the grip of the enemy—watch your back.

Bridge
Apartments

Church

Center

Market

LEGEND

Objectives

- 1 Clear MG nests (3)
- 2 Collect Gammon Grenades
- 3 Knock Out Roving Tiger Tank
- 4 Disable Explosives Plunger
- 5 Disable Radio Equipment
- 6 Assemble and Secure Town Center
- 7 Knock Out Tiger Tank
- 8 Assemble with Airborne and Clear Bridge Surface
- 9 Knock Out Tiger Tank

Secure Zones
(inside light green overlay)

- 1 West of the church
- 2 Southeastern corner of the map, near bridge ramp

Skill Drops

- 1 Land on the balcony
- 2 Land in the church steeple
- 3 Land inside the destroyed room
- 4 Land on the planks between the houses
- 5 Land through the doorway

Weapon Pickups

- 1 M1918 Browning Automatic Rifle
- 2 RPzB 54 Panzerschreck
- Machine Gun Positions
- Health

Miscellaneous

- Ladder

Weapon Loadout

- M1928 Thompson or StG.44
- M1903 Springfield or G43 (if you have the scope upgrade)
- M1911 Colt .45

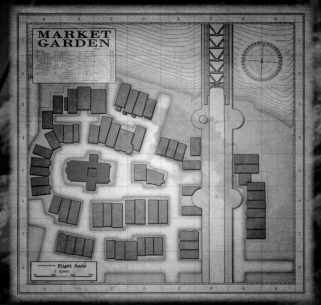

MARKET GARDEN

History

Following the D-day landings and the subsequent breakout from Normandy, the Allied armies had pushed back the Germans for a few months. However, by the end of August, supplies were getting low as intense action on a broad front used up more than could be delivered. It looked like the war would last until 1945. British Field Marshall Bernard Montgomery, the hero of El Alamein, was in command of the forces in the northern part of the Allied line. He devised a plan he felt could quickly move troops across the Rhine and right into Germany—possibly ending the war before Christmas of 1944.

To get to the Rhine in this area, the Allies would have to push across several rivers and water obstacles in Holland. To accomplish this, Montgomery's plan had two main parts. Market would land three airborne divisions (the 82nd, the 101st, and the British 1st) along a highway from the Allied lines to a crossing over the Rhine to capture and hold bridges. Garden, the British component of the operation, required the British 2nd Army to advance along this highway to relieve the paratroops and secure the bridges.

The airborne were dropped on September 17, 1944 and quickly moved toward their targets. Unlike previous operations, they were dropped during daylight, which dramatically increased their accuracy and allowed the paratroopers to assemble quickly once on the ground. The 101st, which was dropped closest to the Allied lines, were able to capture four of their five bridges. The 82nd, the next in line, were able to capture the bridge at Grave and some other of their objectives. However, because they were focused on preventing an enemy armored counterattack, they did not rush to seize the bridge over the Waal at Nijmegan. By the time they tried for this objective, the Germans had reinforced the light defenses. The British dropped at the end of the highway to capture the bridge over the Rhine at Arnhem. However this bridge was much more heavily defended than anticipated. In addition, some elite German units including the 2nd SS Panzer Korps were refitting nearby.

It took the 82nd three days to capture the bridge at Nijmegan and the 2nd British Army was taking longer than anticipated to advance up the two lane highway. Although the British paratroopers at Arnhem tried to hold on, even after being reinforced by Polish airborne troops, they were ordered to begin withdrawing on September 25th. The bridge over the Rhine at Arnhem was "a bridge too far." Although the operation was a failure in that it did not achieve its main objective—a crossing of the Rhine—and the Allies suffered nearly 18,000 casualties as compared to the German's 8,000, those German casualties were elite troops that could have been used during the Battle of the Bulge later that year—and possibly could have contributed to a German victory.

SECURE THE TOWN OF NIJMEGAN

Nijmegan is a city in ruins. All the buildings have suffered heavy damage from bombing and rubble is everywhere. The buildings here are much taller than those in Adanti, and as a result of damage, some walls and even parts of floors are missing. Thus, there are many openings in these buildings through which the enemy can fire down on you. The church, located in the western part of the center, dominates most of the map with its high steeple. From this position, you can snipe down on the streets below.

For the first part of the mission, you must secure the town of Nijmegan. There are some machine gun nests that must be silenced and a tank that must be eliminated. The Germans also have wired the bridge with explosives. Before they can blow the bridge and drop the span into the Waal, you must disable the plunger that will detonate the explosives as well as the radio equipment. Only after you have secured the town of Nijmegan can you go after the bridge and drive the enemy from it. This is not easy because the Germans throw everything they have at you to stop the Allies from capturing this bridge. However, the success of Operation Market Garden relies on your ability to capture this bridge intact—and quickly.

During this mission, you face some of Germany's elite soldiers. In addition to the Waffen SS infantry and officers you have fought already, you also must deal with Waffen SS senior troopers as well as the Third Reich's own paratroopers—the Fallschirmjager infantry. If that's not enough of a challenge, the enemy has positioned Panzergrenadiers on the bridge itself. These soldiers are armed with Panzerfaust rocket launchers—so beware. You can also expect the Germans to have armored units, so don't be surprised if you run into tanks.

LANDING IN NIJMEGAN

You are dropping into a city with many tall buildings—most of which have taken a lot of damage during the war.

This is another day drop, so you have a perfect view of the landscape below you as you jump. Two SZs are set up for you. The first is in the street to the west of the church. Since enemies are all around, it is best to seek cover soon after landing. You can find ammo and health here when needed. The second SZ is in the southeastern part of the map. It, too, has supplies.

The radio equipment and explosives plunger are in the buildings to the north of the church. While they are a priority, it is usually a better idea to go after the Gammon grenades first. A Tiger tank roams around the central building and can cause a lot of trouble for you. The sooner you destroy it, the easier it is to complete the rest of your objectives. The last initial objective is to clear three machine gun nests. Two are in the buildings south of the central area, while the third is to the north.

The SZ by the church is a good place to start the mission.

SKILL DROPS

There are five skill drop locations in Nijmegan. Each of them either puts you near one of your objectives or provides a great position from which you can engage the enemy at a distance and support your fellow paratroopers in securing Nijmegan.

The first skill drop is on a balcony north of the central area. You must land on the balcony itself. To do this, flare shortly after jumping out of the plane, and then push toward the northeast. The balcony is on the building's eastern side, so you must position yourself over the street, then flare as you move on toward the balcony. From this location, you can climb through a window and be just a room away from the northern machine gun nest. However, many enemies are in this building. Stay outside the window using the wall for cover and clear out as many as you can before entering.

2

The second skill drop requires you to land in the church steeple. There is a walkway to the west of the steeple that you can land on. However, do your best to get a greased or flared landing so you are ready to take on the enemy soldier inside the steeple. After it is clear, you can use a sniper rifle to fire down on the streets below, clearing paths for your paratroopers to advance north and south toward the objectives. This makes it easier for you to reach those objectives later on.

3

This skill drop requires you to land inside a destroyed room. This one is located in the northwest. To hit it, you must start flaring and moving north as soon as you jump. You can't drop straight down into this room, so drop over the street and then flare into the room at the last moment. Be ready to take on an enemy because quite a few are in this building. If you botch this landing, you will probably be dead before you can fight back. However, this gives you a great position from which to go after the radio equipment. It is on the same floor, just a few rooms over.

4

This is an interesting skill drop in that you must land on some planks between two buildings in the south. This can be a bit trickier than it looks because you have to avoid landing on the roofs to either side. This requires you to line up your landing a bit earlier and then land right on the plank. Be careful not to turn as you are landing or you may botch it. It is better to go for a flared landing rather than try for a greased landing and risk a botch. From the plank, the southwestern machine gun nest is in the building to the east and just one floor down. You can fire through the destroyed floor and clear this out—then jump down and grab the Gammon grenades.

5

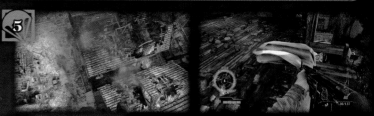

The last skill drop is just to the south of the central area. You must land through a hole in the wall. It is in a wall facing another building, so like the previous skill drop, you must navigate between two buildings and then flare just right to land through the hole. From here, you are just one floor above and a few rooms to the west of the south-eastern machine gun nest. There are usually no enemies in this immediate area when you land, so it is a bit safer than some of the other skill drops and allows you to clear out the southern buildings without exposing yourself to fire from the tank or enemies across the street to the north—unless you get too close to a window.

Tips from the Developer

The Springfield sniper rifle is strongly suggested for this mission. There are many opportunities for snipers in Nijmegan.

NOTE

As with all the missions, you can complete the initial objectives in any order you wish. However, some ways are easier than others. Each objective has multiple ways to approach it and it is usually best to focus on an area of the map rather than completing specific objectives in order. A good order for completing these initial objectives is to land in one of the southern skill drops and clear out the two machine gun nests in these buildings. Grab the Gammon grenades and take out the tank. Then make your way to the north to clear out the last machine gun nest and sabotage the bridge demolitions equipment.

CLEAR THE MACHINE GUN NESTS AND COLLECT THE GAMMON GRENADES

Church

Tiger Tank

Center

Gammon Grenades

Market

LEGEND
Secure Zones

West of the church

Machine Gun Positions   Health

Miscellaneous

Ladder   ← Recommended Path

Weapon Loadout

- M1928 Thompson or StG.44   • M1911 Colt .45

- M1903 Springfield or G43
  (if you have the scope upgrade)

Engage the Germans to the south of the church.

It is usually a good idea to begin in the south. While the skill drop locations put you closer to your objectives, they can also put you right into danger as well. Therefore, if you want to start off safe, land in one of the SZs. The western SZ near the

Continue through the building and then move to the next one, clearing out enemies as you advance.

church is a good place because you have some good cover and some allies to help you out. Quickly take cover behind some rubble, as Germans begin to come out of a building to the south. Fight them off and then rush into the building to make sure it is clear. From there, move out the back through a hole in the wall and enter the building directly to the east from the northern entrance.

TIP

Although you can't bring a Browning automatic rifle at the start of the mission, you can find these weapons at each of the SZs. Another one is near the northern machine gun nest. This weapon is comparable to the StG.44 and superior to a submachine gun.

The fights in the buildings are close and deadly. The rubble provides lots of cover for you as well as your enemies.

Climb a ramp of rubble up to the second floor. Here you must start taking on lots of enemies. The key is to advance cautiously and clear each room as you go. If you rush through, you may leave enemies behind

Clear the room on the other side before crossing the planks.

you and end up surrounded on your own. Therefore, be sure to let your allies advance with you. After you clear out this building, begin engaging Germans in the next building. Clear the way before you move across a plank into the second floor of that building.

TIP

There are three ladders in the southern building to the west of the one containing the southwestern machine gun nest. One takes you up to the third floor, where you can cross to the next building

on another plank. Another ladder goes from the third floor to the fourth floor, where you can find a couple of health kits. Then you can take the third ladder up to the roof. From this vantage, you can snipe at enemies below—even the northern machine gun nest.

The machine gun nest and crate of Gammon grenades are right next to each other.

When it is fairly clear, move across the plank. Immediately to your left is the first machine gun nest. Kill the gunner and any nearby enemies to complete part of that objective. Located in the same room is a supply crate filled with Gammon grenades. When the area is clear, pick up the grenades and then finish clear out this building. Enemies are on the upper floors as well, so watch for them as well as the grenades they drop.

Advance across these planks to the next building.

Clear out all the enemies around this second machine gun nest.

Finish clearing the building you are in, then clear out as much of the easternmost building as you can before crossing over on one of two plank walkways. Finish off any enemies here as well as those manning the machine gun nest. This completes another part of an objective. If you head up the stairs to the third floor, you find a ladder that takes you up to the fourth floor where a couple health kits can be found.

KNOCK OUT THE ROVING TIGER TANK

You should have noticed a Tiger tank driving around the central building in a counterclockwise direction. It keeps driving around and firing from its bow machine gun and its main gun. As long as you don't get too close to

Eliminate the enemies across the street.

the northern windows in the southern buildings, you are fine. However, when the Germans in these buildings are eliminated, the tank will have no problem firing at you.

There are also several Germans in the central building. Wait until the tank goes around that building and then pick off these enemies with your sniper rifle. You can do this from the second floor windows. Clearing out as much of that building as possible will make attacking the tank a bit easier.

Tips from the Developer
Rolling a Gammon grenade so that it lands underneath an enemy tank does more damage than any other attack!

This is a good angle to throw a Gammon grenade at the tank as it comes around the corner. Time it so the grenade is under the tank when it explodes.

When the tank is immobilized, try moving to other windows to avoid taking fire. Keep throwing Gammon grenades until the tank is destroyed.

You must use the Gammon grenades to take out the tank. You can do it from the second floor, dropping grenades down on the tank, or do the same from the ground level. Just be sure you have good cover. While it is more dangerous to attack the tank from the front, it is easier to cause more damage that way. Throw a Gammon grenade in front of the tank's path without cooking it at all. The idea is to have it explode under the tank as it drives over the grenade. If you can do this a couple times, you will immobilize the tank. Then, you can just drop grenades along the sides or try throwing them under the tank. Another grenade or two does the trick. From the second floor, you can try dropping grenades right on top of the tank. You have to cook them for about four seconds so they explode right about when they hit instead of bouncing off and exploding at a distance. This will usually take more grenades.

SABOTAGE THE BRIDGE DEMOLITIONS EQUIPMENT

Radio

Suburbs

Explosive Plunger

Assemble with Airborne

Church

Center

Tiger Tank

LEGEND

Miscellaneous

⬛ Machine Gun Positions   ➕ Health   📔 Ladder

← Recommended Path

Weapon Loadout

- M1928 Thompson or StG.44
- M1903 Springfield or G43 (if you have the scope upgrade)
- M1911 Colt .45

Clear out the interior of the church along with your paratroopers.

Go up the ladder to the steeple and kill the sniper there.

Now that the southern part of the map has been cleared and the tank eliminated, concentrate on your northern objectives. By this time, there is probably be some action around the church, unless you have already cleared it. Help your paratroopers clear out the enemies in the ground floor of the church as well as around the outside. Then climb up to the steeple. Climb ladders inside the church to get up there. Kill the German sniper and then use this position to engage enemies to the north. From the church, you can kill lots of Germans along the pathway leading to the northern building where the radio equipment is as well as enemies within this building. This allows your allies to advance on this position.

Clear out the enemies directly below and along the pathway north.

From the steeple, you can kill many of the enemies at the northern building were the radio is located.

Tips from the Developer

Fight your way into the church to find lots of health.

NOTE

Never assume an area of Nijmegan is clear, just because you already secured it. This is especially true of the central area. After completing an objective, it is common to find more enemies holed up in there. Therefore, as a general rule, always consider this area a threat.

DISABLE THE EXPLOSIVES PLUNGER

As you go past the machine gun nest, throw a grenade through the window so there will be fewer enemies when you get there.

Throw a grenade over the desk to take out the gunner.

Climb down from the church steeple and then go east, staying right next to the buildings on the northern side of the road so the last machine gun can't hit you. Take a left at the corner of the building and go north to find an entrance into this building from the rear. Slowly move up the staircase and throw a cooked grenade into the corner where the machine gun is. That should clear it out.

However, more Germans are to the right at the top of the stairs. Throw another grenade to clear them out or mow them down with your automatic rifle or submachine gun. Then walk over to the explosives plunger and either shoot it or hit it with a melee attack to save bullets. This completes one of your objectives.

Clear out the rest of the enemies in this building, then destroy the explosives plunger.

If you have not picked up a Browning automatic rifle (BAR) yet, you can find one near the northern machine gun nest.

There are probably more Germans directly below you. Go over to the stairs in the same room as the plunger. Throw a grenade so it bounces off the brick wall at the bottom of the stairs and lands back to the left. Then move down to finish off any survivors. That should clear out this building. Time to head to the next objective.

DISABLE THE RADIO EQUIPMENT

This rubble takes you right up to the second floor.

Clear out any remaining enemies on the third floor near the radio.

The radio equipment is in the northwestern building. Approach it from the east and you can climb up to the second floor from a ramp of rubble. A lot of Germans are in this building. However, if you took your time and sniped at them from the church steeple, you may have eliminated enough that your paratroopers were able to kill most of the rest of them. However, if not, you face some close fighting like you did in the southern buildings. Clear out the second floor. Then get to the third floor via stairway or a ladder in the eastern part of the building, near where you entered by the ramp. Clear your way as you advance west. In the northwest corner of this floor, you find the radio equipment. Destroy it all to complete this objective.

Whack the radio equipment with your rifle to destroy it.

ASSEMBLE AND SECURE THE TOWN CENTER

After all the initial objectives have been completed, go back to the center of town. It is a good idea to move to the church and fight from the inside. Use the windows facing the central area for cover as you engage Germans there. When it looks clear, advance on the building, but stay to the north of it. Enemy reinforcements usually arrive from the south and you don't want to get caught inside with them coming at you from different directions. Keep up the pressure and secure this area. Once that is accomplished, one of your paratroopers throws down a green smoke grenade so more of your allies can drop in to help.

Take cover inside the church as you clear out the central area.

Advance and secure the area so you can receive reinforcement.

More Airborne has arrived.

TIP

When clearing the center area, head back to the northern machine gun nest and use the two guns there to help wipe out the enemies below.

KNOCK OUT THE TIGER TANK

Another Tiger has arrived.

Use the sniper rifle to take out some of the soldiers protecting the tank.

As soon as more paratroopers drop in, a Tiger tank breaks through a wall to the east of the central area. Unlike the previous tank, this Tiger stays put and does not drive around. Quickly take cover. Once again, use Gammon grenades to eliminate this threat. The tank is protected by soldiers—and these are elites. The Germans have sent in their Fallschirmjager troops and they will really hurt you if you get in their sights.

Throw Gammon grenades at the side of the tank.

Go to the southern side of the central building and try to pick off these supporting soldiers. Then go after the tank. Lob Gammon grenades at it. To do this, find some cover and then wait for the tank's main gun to fire. Throw a grenade and then duck back behind cover. A good position from which to do this is near the southeastern SZ. You can throw directly at the side of the tank and not have to worry about the bow machine gun or the soldiers protecting the tank. Keep throwing grenades until the tank is a smoking hulk.

TIP

If you need more Gammon grenades, there is a supply crate in the central building.

ASSEMBLE WITH THE AIRBORNE AT THE BRIDGE SURFACE

After the tank is destroyed, there are still some enemy troops near it to try and stop you from getting to the bridge.

Jump down to the apartment metal stairs and clear out the second floor. From here, help take out the Germans below. When it is clear, ascend the metal stairs to the third floor. Clear it if necessary, and then ascend the interior stairway to the third floor, which is adjacent to the surface of the bridge.

Throw grenades through the windows and doors to kill the enemies inside the apartment.

Go up these stairs so you can get a shot at the machine gun.

Blowing up the Tiger tank opens a new pathway, allowing you to approach the bridge. However, before rushing through, clear out the enemies behind the tank. This allows your allies to advance. As you move forward, look for some metal stairs leading up toward the bridge. Follow the stairs to the top and then continue toward the apartment to the east, where the Germans are defending. From the catwalk, you can get a good shot at the machine gun on the second floor. Stay there and engage all the Germans who try to man the machine gun or move to engage your paratroopers below.

CLEAR AND SECURE THE BRIDGE

Panzergrenadiers with Panzerschreck take out the column of tanks.

After you arrive at the bridge surface, a column of Sherman tanks arrives. However, they are quickly destroyed by German Panzergrenadiers armed with Panzerschreck on the bridge. These rocket launchers are equally deadly to infantry, so take cover. Use the sandbags to hide behind, then pop up and snipe at the enemy. First, eliminate the German gunner in the pillbox because he can cause a lot of damage to your allies with his machine gun. Then, go after the rest of the German infantry. Kill as many as you can from this position and then climb up the stairs to the top level of the apartments.

You have a good field of fire for sniping. Silence that machine gun first.

While sniping, be careful not to stay in scope sight too long. It is an easy way to get killed. Take a shot, and then duck down. Pop up to look for a target, and then zoom in to take the shot.

Take up a position near the machine gun, but let one of your allies man it. Then start picking off the enemy soldiers on the bridge. The Panzergrenadiers are your main targets. Because the rockets fired by the Panzerschreck travel slower

The paratrooper on the machine gun helps cover you.

than a bullet, you can actually fire right after they do and still have time to duck down under cover. You can do a lot of damage to the enemy by sniping from the machine gun nest in the apartment. This allows your allies to advance out onto the bridge.

Watch for Panzergrenadiers on elevated catwalks along the sides of the bridge. If you are focusing on the road level, you can easily miss them.

Head down to the surface of the bridge and then rush across to the opposite side.

After you have eliminated all the enemies you can see from this position, go down the ramp onto the bridge surface and rush toward the pillbox. Take cover behind barrels along the way to see if you can snipe anyone else. Advance a bit farther and try again. By the time you get to the pillbox, you should have eliminated most of the enemy infantry on the bridge. Therefore, pick up a Panzerschreck just to the north of the pillbox. You can swap the sniper rifle for this rocket launcher.

Pick up this Panzerschreck.

KNOCK OUT THE TIGER TANK

Move around the bus and rush for the truck on the left side to use as cover from the tank.

There is one more tank to destroy to complete this mission. Because it is hidden behind civilian vehicles, you cannot take long shots at it from the bridge surface. You have to come at it from the side, using the vehicles for cover. Just watch

You can only hit the front from the elevated platforms.

For a longer-range shot, you can climb up onto one of the elevated platforms on the right side of the bridge. Just be sure to take cover behind one of the steel girders between the tank's main gunshots. It will take several hits

Continue around to the rear of the truck so you can get a side shot on the Tiger.

out for the bow machine gun and time your shots to avoid the tank's gun. As before, aim for the sides, which have less armor than the front. You also need to watch out for enemy infantry around the tank. It is best to take them out first. Use your BAR or throw grenades to destroy them, then concentrate on the tank.

because you are firing at the front of the tank. As soon as the tank is knocked out, the mission is a success.

TIP

If you still have some Gammon grenades, you can lob them over the bus at the tank on the other side. This keeps you safe while you destroy the tank. Practice with regular grenades to get the angle of the throw and the timing just right before using a Gammon grenade. If you need more of these grenades, a crate of them waits along the left side of the bridge.

The bridge is secure and Allied units immediately start crossing.

OPERATION VARSITY

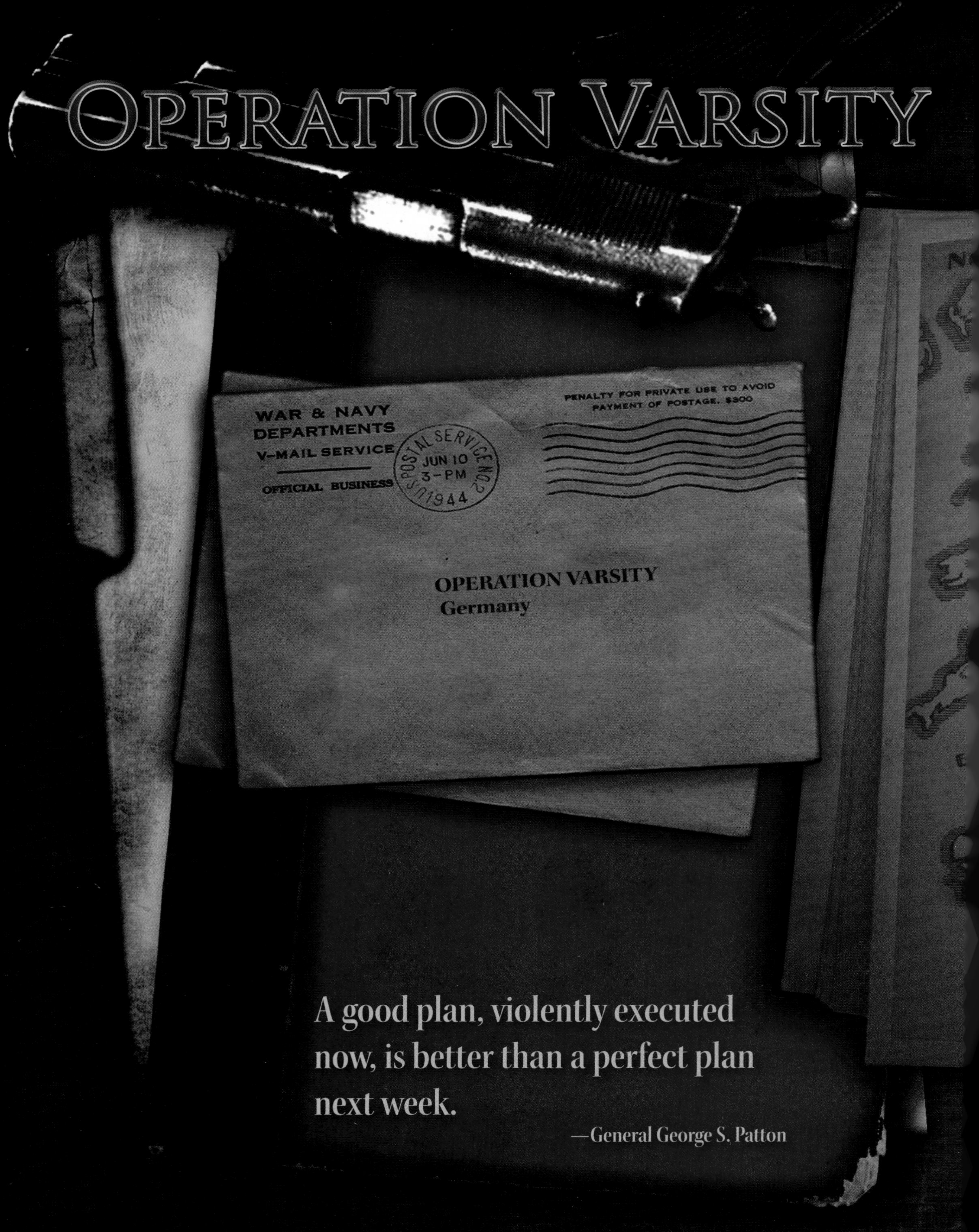

WAR & NAVY
DEPARTMENTS
V-MAIL SERVICE
——————
OFFICIAL BUSINESS

U.S. POSTAL SERVICE NO.2
JUN 10
3-PM
1944

PENALTY FOR PRIVATE USE TO AVOID
PAYMENT OF POSTAGE. $300

OPERATION VARSITY
Germany

A good plan, violently executed
now, is better than a perfect plan
next week.

—General George S. Patton

25 March 1945

Supporting the advance across the Rhine was an air assault, by two airborne divisions, the U.S. 17th and the British 6th, a combined force of more than 20,000 troops. The 17th was the newest American airborne division in the ETO (European Theater of Operations), having arrived on the Continent in December. The men experienced their baptism of fire in the Battle of the Bulge and gave a good account of themselves. They, like those in my division, made practice jumps in France for a possible airborne mission.

On 24 March the 17th took off from the marshalling areas in France and landed in Germany behind enemy lines at 1010. They encountered unexpectedly strong enemy resistance. On the first day, they suffered more than 900 casualties: 159 killed in action, 522 wounded, and 250 missing. Many troop carrier planes and gliders were also destroyed or damaged. Given the tactical situation and the status of German forces, the question was asked, Was the airborne assault necessary? And was it worth the casualties the airborne forces suffered?

—James Megellas, *All the Way to Berlin*
(New York: Random House), 289

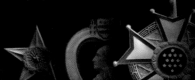

MEDAL OF HONOR
AIRBORNE

Briefing

Attention Airborne. This is Operation Varsity. We are going to be dropping into Germany. Our enemy is about to collapse, but that doesn't mean he's weak. Our first target is a factory. The Air Force has bombed it for weeks, but a month's worth of war matériel remains undamaged. There is a panzer tank assembly building where local resistance reports a railgun is inside. If you find it, you know what to do. The enemy has several tanks ready for delivery to the front line. Make sure they never leave the rail yard. Finally, there is a chemical munitions building where they build antiaircraft shells. A large supply is inside. Make sure those shells are never used. This is a simple mission. If it can shoot you or be shot at you, destroy it.

Munitions Chemical Plant

Rail Yard

Loading Docks

Steel Mill

Tank Factory

LEGEND

Objectives

⚔ Destroy the Tanks on the Railcars (3)

⚔ Destroy the Munitions Stockpile

⚔ Destroy the Railgun

⚔ Sabotage the Tank Factory Control Room

⚔ Destroy the Pressure Valves (2)

⚔ Assemble with the Airborne at the Steel Mill

⚔ Clear and Secure the Entrance to the Rail Yard

⚔ Destroy the Panzerzug Cannon Cars (2)

⚔ Destroy the Panzerzug Engine

Secure Zones
(inside light green overlay)

🏭 Near tank factory

🏭 On top of the loading docks

Skill Drops

1 Land on top of the fuel tank

2 Land through the doorway

3 Land on top of the catwalk

4 Land on top of the catwalk

5 Land on top of the flatbed train car

Weapon Pickups

1 M1903 Springfield Sniper Rifle

2 M1903 Springfield Sniper Rifle

3 C96 Mauser Pistol

Machine Gun Positions

Health

Miscellaneous

📖 Ladder

← Recommended Path

Weapon Loadout

- M1928 Thompson or StG.44
- M1903 Springfield or G43 (if you already have the scope upgrade)
- M1911 Colt .45

FACTORY
Flight Route
1:15.000

History A little before 1000 hours on March 24, a vast armada of aircraft began flying over Germany in a wave that lasted more than two and a half hours. An impressive fleet of 1,996 transports and 1,348 gliders carried more than 21,000 American and British troops into battle. They were escorted by 889 fighters, though no German planes appeared to mess with the operation. For three days previous, Allied bombers had hit targets throughout Germany and Allied artillery pounded enemy anti-aircraft batteries just prior to the airborne drops. Operation Varsity had begun.

Those troops who dropped at the beginning faced little resistance. However, as the drops continued, later paratroopers began to take anti-aircraft fire. However, the operation was a success. Despite some heavy casualties, both the Americans and British seized all of their first-day objectives. This was a result of some heroic actions by the paratroopers of the 17th Airborne Division.

Private George J. Peters, of the 507th Regiment, landed with his stick of paratroopers and immediately came under fire from a German machine gun as well as riflemen. Peters charged the machine gun, which was seventy-five yards away. He was knocked down by gunfire halfway there, but continued to charge until he was close enough to destroy the machine gun position with a hand grenade before dying from his wounds.

A member of the 513th regiment, PFC Stuart S. Stryker, was advancing with his company near a complex of buildings when they began to take heavy fire. With his platoon pinned down, Stryker rose up and led a charge against the buildings that resulted in the capture of more than 200 German prisoners. Stryker was cut down by enemy fire as he neared the buildings.

Both of these brave paratroopers were posthumously awarded the Medal of Honor for their actions.

SECURE THE FACTORY DROP ZONE

If you thought you had been through some tough missions, this one is the toughest yet. You are dropping during daylight right into the middle of an enemy-held facility. Expect to come under fire from snipers even before you land. Once on the ground, you must begin going after your objectives. The tanks you must destroy are in the eastern area known as the rail yard. The tank factory, where two of your objectives await, is in the north. The munitions stockpile is located in the munitions chemical plant in the southern part of the map. Finally, the pressure valves are up near the large tanks in the loading docks area.

This factory complex can be a nightmare. There are tall buildings, conveyors, catwalks, and towers. All are perfect for snipers, so even if you think you are safe, a shot from up above will remind you of the constant danger during this mission. To complete some of your objectives, you must venture into the two factory buildings. Both are filled with enemy soldiers and the mission combines close combat with long-range fire in the large open areas.

During this mission, you face the most elite of the enemy forces. Even the common soldiers here are Waffen senior troopers or Fallschirmjager. You also face the most powerful enemy in the game—the Nazi Storm Elite. This soldier carries a light machine gun and can take a lot of hits before he is killed.

LANDING IN THE FACTORY

During this drop, your transport plane takes heavy fire. You are one of the few to make it off.

This map offers number places to land. Since snipers are up high and soldiers are on the ground, it is safest to land at one of the two SZs. Both provide a good place to begin the mission, provide some allies right at the start, and also have cover. As soon as you land, find some cover while you get your bearings.

If you land at the northern SZ, you are close to the tank factory and can go for the two objectives in there first. The rail yard with the tanks is just to the east, offering another possible initial objective. On the other hand, the southern SZ provides a good place to go after either the munitions stockpile in the southern building or the pressure valves in the loading dock area.

Tips from the Developer

Land by the green smoke in the upper section of the loading docks. Take the ladder up, then take the second ladder straight ahead to reach the roof of the metal shack. From this location, you can engage the snipers in the rail yard from above—essentially negating their vertical advantage.

NOTE

Like most of the missions, it really does not matter which objectives you choose to go after first. Obviously, the only two you should do together are destroying the railgun and sabotaging the control room, as both are in the tank factory. However, the rest is up to you. This walkthrough merely covers them in the order listed in the game.

The northern SZ is a good place to land. It is close to three of your objectives.

SKILL DROPS

There are five skill drop locations in the factory complex. Each gives you great access to an objective or provides a spot from which you can snipe the enemy below you to help your allies on the ground. Unfortunately, many of these skill drop locations are exposed, so expect to come under enemy fire and do your best not to botch the landing—which can be tough since the terrain is uneven.

The first skill drop is on top of the central tank. This can be a tough one to grease since stepping off the raised center can result in a botched landing. It is better to flare this landing since you want to bring up your weapon as quickly as possible. A sniper is positioned on the large tank just to the west; he starts shooting at you before you can even touch down. After landing here, you must climb down the ladder located to the east to access other areas. From there, you can easily go after the pressure valves or take the catwalk into the second floor of the tank factory.

The second skill drop requires you to land through a doorway on the second floor of the munitions chemical plant. Either flare or grease this landing so you are ready to fight as soon as you enter the building. From this location, you can quickly begin engaging enemies inside the southern building and go after the objective inside—destroying the munitions stockpile. As soon as you start the fight, your allies quickly join you to help take on the Germans.

This skill drop requires you to move to the east and land on a catwalk over the rail yard. This is not a tough landing to stick and you can even grease it fairly easily. However, be ready to take out the sniper in the shack to the southeast. He starts shooting at you as soon as you land, and could kill you if you botch this landing. From this position, you can engage enemies below in the rail yard or move west to go after the other objectives.

This is another catwalk landing. However, this is a tough one to get. It is located under pipes and other catwalks. You have to move north toward the tank factory, and then turn around to face south. Flare as you continue south to slip under the pipes and make it onto the catwalk. Be ready for enemies in this area, since they come at you from the west. From this skill drop location, it is easy to get to the pressure valves. Or you can take the catwalk over to the top floor of the tank factory and begin working on those objectives.

The final skill drop requires you to land on a flatbed car in the rail yard. The car is actually on an overpass just to the east of the munitions plant. As soon as you start to drop, begin moving southeast and flare so you can reach the location. Landing on it is not that difficult. As with most of this mission's drop spots, here you come under immediate fire. Jump down to the west side of the flatcar for cover, then engage several snipers to the east. From here, you can clear out most of the rail yard and allow your allies below to mop up.

DESTROY THE TANKS ON THE RAILCARS

These snipers have a bead on the SZ. Eliminate them quickly.

The tanks in the rail yard are as good a place to start as any for this mission. Land safely in the northern SZ. Duck down quickly and get your bearings. A couple snipers wait to the east in a box car up on an overpass. Use your sniper rifle to get rid of them first. Also, watch for other enemies that might come after you from the direction of the tank factory.

Stay between the wall and these shacks. Stop at the gap to engage snipers to the south.

Now move east, staying as close to the northern wall as you can. You come across a couple of shacks. Stay to the north of them as well. However, when you get to the gap between them, stop. Peek around the corner while looking south to locate a sniper inside the conveyer buildings up high. Shoot him with your sniper rifle.

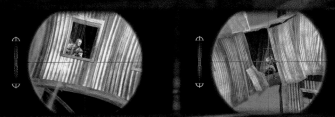

The snipers can be tough to hit because they like to take cover—especially when you point a sniper rifle in their direction. Just be patient and they eventually reveal themselves. Be sure to aim for the head so you get a one-shot kill.

Snipers usually give themselves away with the glare of the sun reflecting off their scope. If you see a bright speck, take cover quick. You can also see the path of incoming bullets. So if you start taking fire, look for these telltale signs to locate an enemy sniper.

This machine gun position can prevent your allies from advancing down in the rail yard.

Snipe at the Germans below to support the paratroopers during the firefight.

Continue behind the second shack. Once again, stop to peek around the corner. Yet another sniper is to the south. This one is in an elevated shack below a catwalk skill drop. Eliminate this threat. Now go south for a bit, and then quickly move up the steel stairway to take out a soldier manning a machine gun at the top. Another is inside the building, so eliminate him as well. Now you can use the machine gun to engage the Germans below so your allies can advance. However, it is usually better to stick with the sniper rifle and take out as many enemies as possible to the south and southeast. Scan the entire area through your scope to make sure it is clear. A machine gun to the southwest can cause you trouble later, so kill the gunner now.

This sniper was right above you on the roof.

After you have engaged all visible targets, go down the stairs. However, before rushing out into the rail yard, kill the sniper on top of the roof of the building where you just were. Now proceed over to the shacks along the eastern side. Clear them of any remaining Germans so they don't shoot you in the back while you are completing your objective here. As soon as this area is safe, it is time to blow up the three tanks. Climb up onto the flatbed cars using the small ladders at the ends and place a charge on the rear of each tank. Now move on to the next objective.

TIP

You can also destroy the tanks with Gammon grenades. It just takes one thrown directly under the tank. While you begin the mission with some of these powerful grenades, you can find more in the shack above the machine gun along the western side of the rail yard. There is also a sniper in this shack, so kill him if you haven't already done so.

DESTROY THE MUNITIONS STOCKPILE

All the tanks you must blow up are on flatbed cars.

One down, two to go.

Ascend these stairs to the second level of the plant.

Tips from the Developer
Make sure you are crouched while planting explosives so you are a tougher target for the enemy to hit.

The munitions stockpile is in an underground level of the chemical munitions plant. However, the only way to gain entrance is to take a steel stairway up to the second level. Although there is a doorway at the top, don't go in just yet.

This ladder takes you to the roof and provides a better position from which to enter this building.

Instead, climb up the nearby ladder to the roof where you can meet up with some more paratroopers.

Snipe the Germans on the lower levels.

Enter the plant through a doorway on the roof and immediately take cover behind some corrugate metal along a railing. This protects you from gunfire from the lower levels. Your allies usually cover the stairs to the left for you while you snipe at the Germans below. The key target is the machine gun directly ahead of you on the second level. As you clear out all the enemies you can see, advance toward the stairs and fire at enemies below and to the south. When it looks pretty clear below, head down the stairs. Be ready for an enemy to pop out.

The stairs to the ground level are in the western part of the building. As you descend, watch for enemies.

Advance through this building to get on the flank of the machine gun.

After clearing the second level, begin to shoot enemies on the ground level. A machine gun stands along the eastern side, so be sure to kill the gunner before descending the stairs at the western end. When on the ground level, stay to the south and advance from cover to cover. You still must watch out for the machine gun. Move through the room in the southeast corner, which allows you to advance toward the big gun under cover. Emerge from the door at the opposite end to flank the machine gun.

Climb down the ladder to get to the bottom of the shaft—and the munitions stockpile.

Peek around corners and use grenades to kill enemies behind cover.

Directly behind the machine gun is an elevator shaft. The elevator is down, so you must climb down a ladder. Because the ladder does not reach all the way down, you must drop the rest of the way, but you won't be able to get back up this way. Therefore, make sure you have all the ammo you need before descending. The shaft takes you down to the underground level where the munitions stockpile is. In addition to lots of shells, you also find lots of enemies. You are now in a close-quarters fight. The main tactic is to stay low and peek around corners. Watch for enemies because they even fire around corners at you, and do not give you much of a target to shoot at. This is when grenades come in handy.

Keep your magazine full in case the Germans try to rush you in a group.

Keep an eye on your compass to see where the enemies are waiting to ambush you. Advance cautiously through this maze o shells. You eventual reach the place where you can set the charge. Before doing so, clear out the passageway past this point that leads to some stairs. That is your way out. Place the charge, then rush up those stairs to get out of the munitions plant before it all blows up. Don't worry about the door at the top of the stairs. The concussion from the explosion blows it out by the time you get there.

Usually at least one enemy is back by the place where you plant the charge.

Run up the stairs to get out of the underground level before the roof collapses.

DESTROY THE RAILGUN AND SABOTAGE THE TANK FACTORY CONTROL ROOM

Clear the area outside the factory, including the machine gun.

The Germans come at you as you enter the tank factory. Keep your magazine full and be ready to toss a quick grenade to disperse them.

The tank factory contains two of your objectives. Enter through the main door on the ground level, just to the west of the northern SZ. Use your automatic rifle or submachine gun to take on the enemies guarding this area. Wait for your allies to catch up, then advance to the east, using cover as you go. More Germans are near a shack in the southeastern corner of the factory. Eliminate them and then enter the shack if you need some health.

Tips from the Developer

Here is another way to complete the munitions stockpile objective. Grease your landing when dropping onto the second floor catwalk of the chemical plant and then jump onto and over the barrels next to the railing just in front of your location. You end up on the first floor on top of a vat. Then, quickly sprint south around the tanks to the elevator shaft. You can make it into the basement with one or two bars of health—and without having to fight all the enemies inside the large main room of this building.

NOTE

If you move due north after exiting the chemical munitions plant, you end up at the northern SZ, where you can stock up on health and ammo. Then you are in a perfect spot to enter the tank factory. Watch out for Germans along the way.

TIP

You can enter the tank factory from the ground level or by taking the metal stairs and catwalks from the loading docks area into this building's upper level. If you have just completed the pressure valves objective, or parachuted onto the catwalks, go in through the upper level where you can snipe the enemies below. Otherwise, fight your way in through the ground floor. However, once inside, find ladders to get to the upper level.

Ladders near this shack take you up to the high catwalks.

Meet up with your allies near the upper entrance so they can help you get through to your objectives.

While you can stay on the ground level, it is better to gain a height advantage. Climb up the ladder near the shack, then walk across the roof to another ladder that takes you to the upper catwalks. Move west to clear the pathway to the upper entrance and meet up with some allies who (hopefully) have parachuted in through this opening. Now go back toward the ladder and follow the catwalk around to the north and then west.

try to clear it out before dropping down yourself. Eliminate any remaining enemies inside the control room and then sabotage the controls by shooting them or using a melee attack.

Destroy these controls.

TIP

If you need some health, go south out of the control room then turn left. A door opens as you approach. Several Germans are on the other side, so kill them all. Then, move in and restore your health. This room is a dead-end, so return to the control room.

Take cover behind crates as you fight along the catwalks.

This catwalk goes over the control room. Drop a few grenades in to eliminate some of the enemies.

Fight along the northern catwalk as you continue moving west. Use the crates for cover during this often-intense engagement. About midway into the factory, you see a catwalk that leads south, but which has been damaged. This hole actually drops right into the factory control room. You can move south on this catwalk and take cover behind some of the railings as you shoot at enemies to the west. Then, drop some grenades down into the control room to

Blow the safe to get the new pistol.

While in the control room, you see a safe. Throw a Gammon grenade at it to blow it open. Pick up a C96 Mauser pistol inside. Trade out your M1911 Colt .45 for this German pistol. It has some really cool upgrades. Exit the control room and go to the west again.

Tips from the Developer
Try clearing out the tank factory first so you can pick up the Mauser ASAP. If you then use it as you go through the loading docks and then the chemical plant, you will have an almost fully upgraded Mauser to finish up the rest of mission. This fully automatic weapon with unlimited ammo is awesome.

The railgun is down below. Before going after it, continue fighting the Germans who arrive to stop you. The crates in the northwestern part of the catwalks provide some good cover. When this area is clear of enemies, jump up on one of the crates, and then drop down onto the railgun. Or, follow the catwalks all the way around to the south to get to the ground floor. Set a charge on the breech of the railgun to destroy it and complete the second objective in the tank factory. A large door south of the railgun opens so you can exit the factory there instead of having to go all the way back to your entrance point.

Finish off many of the Germans on the catwalks as you hold the position in the northwest.

The railgun is directly below this position.

 **TIP**

If you want to destroy the railgun while still fighting enemies, drop a couple of Gammon grenades into the depression by the breech of the gun. That does the job without having to get down to the gun and expose yourself to enemy fire.

DESTROY THE PRESSURE VALVES

If you approach the catwalks in the loading docks area from the northwest, you can flank this machine gun position.

The two pressure valves that you must destroy are near the large storage tanks in the loading docks area. If you are coming from the tank factory, move west and then climb up some metal stairs. This allows you to come up on the flank of the machine gun guarding the lower catwalks. Don't use the machine gun, but take up a position with cover near it as you engage the Germans who come at you. Hold here until your allies can join you.

TIP

Look for places on the railings that have metal sheets that you can use for cover. They make good places to stop and fight.

Place the charge on the breech.

As you exit the factory, watch out for Germans on the catwalks in the loading docks area.

Climb up this ladder.

Take cover behind these pipes as you clear out the catwalks.

The first pressure valve is in this shack.

Now climb up the ladder to the north of the machine gun to the next level of catwalks. Quickly take cover behind some large pipes and engage the Germans to the south near a shack with one of the pressure valves inside. Keep up the assault until you eliminate them. Then advance to the east, fighting enemies until you link up with your allies. Together, return to the shack and place a charge on the pressure valve. Get out before it blows.

TIP

It is important to stay with your allies in this area. They are great for protecting you while you are planting charges and so forth. If you try to do this solo, you will have many enemies gunning for you.

Lob a grenade into the second shack to blow up the soldiers inside.

The second pressure valve is in the east up on a higher level. Backtrack around to the northeast to find some stairs leading up. Follow them around to another shack. A couple snipers are inside, so toss in a grenade,

Put the charge here to blow up this pressure valve.

then rush in to finish off any survivors. Don't stay out in the open on the catwalks around here because a couple more snipers are on top of the storage tanks to the northwest. Use a charge to blow up the second pressure valve. One more objective is now complete.

ASSEMBLE WITH THE AIRBORNE AT THE STEEL MILL, AND CLEAR AND SECURE THE ENTRANCE TO THE RAIL YARD

Now that all the initial objectives have been secured, more paratroopers are dropping in. Meet with them in the southwestern part of the loading docks area.

From the top of the shack, you can snipe at the machine gun as well as the enemies fighting against your allies.

As more airborne troops start dropping in, Germans emerge from the steel mill in the southwest. If you are already up near the pressure valves, you have a height advantage you can use to your benefit. Climb up the ladder onto the roof of the western pressure valve shack. From here, snipe at the machine gun to the west as well as the enemies below to the south. This helps support your allies down below.

After killing all the enemies you can from the shack roof, go down to the catwalks and descend to the ground level to finish off the remaining Germans. Advance to the gate to the steel mill rail yard to receive new orders.

Advance to this gate.

The Panzerzug arrives, as well as this new threat.

Take cover and fire at the Nazi Storm Elite solider while he is reloading his light machine gun.

As your allies open the gate to the rail yard, an enemy armored train, or Panzerzug, rolls to a stop. German troops disembark. One soldier stands out from among the rest—a Nazi Storm Elite. Armed with an MG42 light machine gun, this is one tough enemy. Quickly take cover behind some crates before you are gunned down. When you can, move back to your left for better cover. You also find some crates with health kits, weapons ammo, and explosives. Don't use them until you need them or are leaving this area.

Destroy Panzerzug Engine and Cannon Cars

Use the sniper rifle to engage enemies at long range.

When you have good cover, begin engaging the closest enemies. Then switch to your sniper rifle and go after those at a distance and on the catwalks above. Your top priority is the Nazi Storm Elites—actually, two of them are in this area. Listen for their light machine gun fire to determine where they are. It is best to engage them at long range. They can take a lot of hits, but are vulnerable to head shots. Make two or three head shots on these monsters and they go down.

The Nazi Storm Elites are tough to kill. Their machine guns have a lot of firepower and are deadly—especially at close range. The best tactic is to get away from them. If they get too close, throw a grenade. Although it does not kill them, it either wounds them or gets them to move away, giving you a chance to seek new cover and hopefully put some distance between you and these killing machines. While behind cover, listen to their gunfire. When the elites stop to reload, take your shots. Go for the head if you have a sniper rifle or the body for less accurate weapons. A couple of Gammon grenades can also do the trick.

Put this machine gun out of business.

NOTE

Many Germans are in this last area. They do not all come at once. Therefore, even if you think you have completely cleared it, use caution still or one may come up behind you in a deadly surprise.

As soon as it is clear, move up the stairs on the left and move along the catwalks. A machine gun is positioned above the train's rear half. Neutralize its threat by killing the gunner. Then, advance, clearing the catwalks as you go. You do not have to kill all the enemies to complete this objective—only destroy the train. However, the fewer Germans around, the easier it is to accomplish your task.

If you did not kill the snipers on top of the large storage tanks, they may fire down on you.

A sniper lurks at the far end of this area over the rear of the Panzerzug. Watch for the glint of his scope.

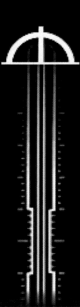

You can plant a charge on the train compartments or throw Gammon grenades. They must land inside to destroy the train.

The Panzerzug has three parts: two cannon cars with the engine in the middle. Each must be destroyed individually. There are two ways you can blow up the engine and cannon cars. Compartments on top of each are open. Climb up onto the catwalks that go over the train, then jump down on the train and plant an explosive charge in each compartment. Another way is to throw Gammon grenades into the compartments. Practice with regular grenades to learn the right angle and strength of the throw. It takes only a single Gammon grenade to destroy each section of the Panzerzug. When all three have been destroyed, the mission is complete.

Mission accomplished!

DER FLAKTURM

WAR & NAVY
DEPARTMENTS
V—MAIL SERVICE

OFFICIAL BUSINESS

PENALTY FOR PRIVATE USE TO AVOID
PAYMENT OF POSTAGE. $300

U.S. POSTAL SERVICE N.º 2
JUN 10
3 – PM
1944

**Der Flakturm
Germany**

"Courage is fear holding on a
minute longer."

—General George S. Patton

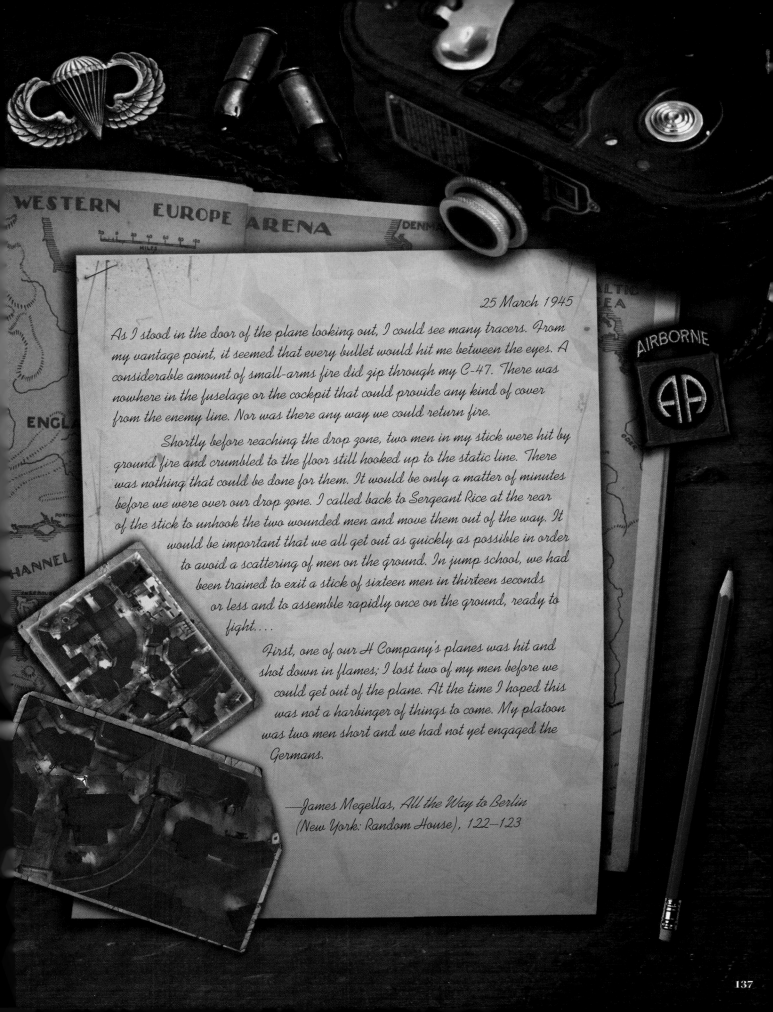

25 March 1945

As I stood in the door of the plane looking out, I could see many tracers. From my vantage point, it seemed that every bullet would hit me between the eyes. A considerable amount of small-arms fire did zip through my C-47. There was nowhere in the fuselage or the cockpit that could provide any kind of cover from the enemy line. Nor was there any way we could return fire.

Shortly before reaching the drop zone, two men in my stick were hit by ground fire and crumbled to the floor still hooked up to the static line. There was nothing that could be done for them. It would be only a matter of minutes before we were over our drop zone. I called back to Sergeant Rice at the rear of the stick to unhook the two wounded men and move them out of the way. It would be important that we all get out as quickly as possible in order to avoid a scattering of men on the ground. In jump school, we had been trained to exit a stick of sixteen men in thirteen seconds or less and to assemble rapidly once on the ground, ready to fight. . . .

First, one of our H Company's planes was hit and shot down in flames; I lost two of my men before we could get out of the plane. At the time I hoped this was not a harbinger of things to come. My platoon was two men short and we had not yet engaged the Germans.

—James Megellas, *All the Way to Berlin*
(New York: Random House), 122–123

Briefing

Alright, airborne. Two days ago the Allies began Operation Varsity. Thus far we have mastered the enemy on every turn. However, there is one target that refuses to fall. Our objective is the monstrosity called a flak tower. It is a city in itself; the enemy's last bastion of defense. For our bombers to hit it, we must first take out its defenses. There are several AA emplacements on the roof. All guns must be destroyed. Enemy armor patrols the ground-floor entrances. When the area is secure, get inside and figure out how to bring it down. We are sending in demolitions teams to take care of that, so assist them in any way possible. This mission is the final test of your skills and courage. I have never seen the Airborne quit, and I expect I never will. See you all back home.

LEGEND

Objectives

1 Destroy Artillery Guns (3)

2 Destroy AA Guns (4)

3 Eliminate Enemies on Halftracks (3)

4 Disable Ammunition Lift Controls (4th Floor)

5 Disable Ammunition Lift Controls (2nd Floor)

6 Assemble at Main Control Room (3rd Floor)

7 Assemble with Engineers in Ammunition Storage

8 Escape Flak Tower

9 Destroy Flak Tower

Secure Zones

1 On the roof

2 On the outside of the lower gun level

3 In courtyard on ground level

Skill Drops

1 Land through the doorway

2 Land in the secret entrance

3 Land on the scaffolding outside the doorway

4 Land in the secret entrance

5 Land through the doorway

Weapon Loadout

- Browning Automatic Rifle or StG.44

- Mauser

- M1903 Springfield or G43 (if you have the scope upgrade)

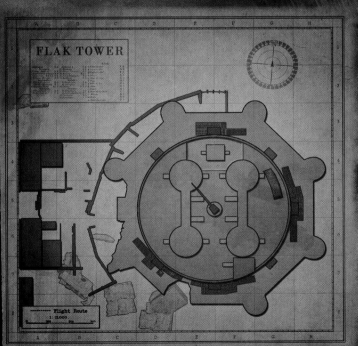

FLAK TOWER

Flight Route
1: 11.000

History

Flak Towers

Nazi Germany actually built several flak towers similar to the one in this mission. Their purpose was to force Allied bombers away from their coverage area and help protect vital parts of important cities including Berlin and Hamburg, Germany, as well as Vienna, Austria.

With reinforced concrete walls eight feet thick, these fortresses could withstand hits from most Allied bombs and only a direct hit from a specially designed bomb could penetrate—though bombing was less accurate during WWII than the laser- and satellite-guided bombs of today.

The teeth of the flak towers were its weapons. Most were armed with four twin-mounted 128mm Flak 40 antiaircraft guns. These guns could fire shells weighing nearly 60 pounds up to 35,000 feet in the air at a rate of 20 rounds per minute. In addition, smaller antiaircraft guns were mounted around the tower's periphery.

Flak towers were not only built to survive air attacks, but could hold out during essential sieges. They were stocked with plenty of ammunition and food. However, since civilians often took shelter in these towers, supplies rarely lasted as long as intended. In fact, the only way the Russians were able to capture them during the fight for Berlin was to wait for those inside to run out of food and surrender.

Many of these flak towers are still around today. Because of their massive construction, it would cost too much to demolish them, if it could be done without damaging surrounding structures. These fortresses were built to last and they most likely will for decades to come.

SECURE THE FLAK TOWER

The flak tower is an impregnable fortress filled with lots of heavy weapons and scores of enemy soldiers. Any other type of soldier would consider this a suicide mission. However, you are Airborne, and the impossible is what you are trained to do. Your objectives take you from the top of the flak tower to the ground, as you engage enemies on each and every level. Your initial objectives require you to destroy both the artillery guns as well as the antiaircraft batteries defending the flak tower. You must also disable the ammunition lift that carries shells from the underground storage area to the guns on top, then carries the empty shell casings back down. Finally, you must neutralize the German halftracks protecting the ground entrances to the flak tower so additional American troops can enter.

While most of this mission takes place indoors, you face a lot of ranged combat in addition to close-quarters fighting. Be ready for both. Luckily, the flak tower contains many health kits as well as ammo and weapons; you need all of them. Be on the lookout for things to pick up that will help you achieve your objectives.

Only the most trained and veteran soldiers are guarding the flak tower. Therefore, you must use all the skills and abilities you have developed during past missions to help you survive and emerge victorious. In the previous mission, you faced a couple of Nazi Storm Elite soldiers. Expect to see more of them in the flak tower.

You can land anywhere to start the mission. However, for the first time playing on the flak tower, it is best to land on the roof and work your way down to the ground, clearing as you go. To play the most challenging way, land on the ground level and fight your way in through the front door.

LANDING ON THE FLAK TOWER

As your plane approaches the target, it is latterly cut in half by the enemy flak. Quickly get your bearings and prepare to land.

This jump is the most dangerous you have ever done. When you are forced from the plane, you take enemy fire from snipers. The longer you are in the air, the more chance you have of getting hit. There are three secure zones. One is on the rooftop of the flak tower. The second is on the outside of the lower gun level. The final SZ is down in the town at ground level. At each location, you find crates of ammo, health kits, and explosives.

Both of the SZs on the flak tower quickly come under fire. However, there is nearby cover and you can easily recover from a botched landing without being killed. The ground level SZ is a bit safer because you land in an area with a tall concrete wall between you and the flak tower; however, snipers on the tower's scaffolding can still fire on you unless you land right next to the wall.

The SZ on the rooftop is a good place to land for this mission.

SKILL DROPS

There are five skill drop locations in Essen.

This skill drop requires you to land through a doorway into the upper gun level of the flak tower. This is a landing you want to grease if possible because Germans inside the tower begin firing on you. You land right next to one of the artillery guns, allowing you to start on one of the objectives right away. This is a fairly easy skill drop to hit. Head toward it, flaring as necessary, then as you are about to hit, move forward so you can grease the landing.

This second skill drop is tougher to hit. It is an opening on the side of the flak tower. Move over so you drop alongside the tower, right above this opening. Move forward as you are about to pass by the opening to land inside. From the passage you land in, move along some catwalks into a room filled with ammo, health, and explosives, as well as weapons including a recoilless rifle. Take a ladder up from this room, then move across to another ladder. Now you're inside the upper control room with one of your objectives.

The third skill drop forces you to land on the scaffolding outside the doorway on the side of the flak tower. This anding is not too tough. From here, enter the flak tower at the upper shaft level.

This skill drop is another secret opening in the side of the flak tower. From here, you emerge onto a short catwalk with some cover and a great place to snipe at enemies on the middle shaft level of the tower. This is a tough one to achieve because there is scaffolding right above it. Drop away from the tower so you don't hit the scaffolding, then flare and move forward underneath the scaffolding to land inside the opening.

The last skill drop requires you to land through a doorway on the third floor of the southern building. The doorway faces east, so when you begin to fall, turn and move toward this building. Stay to the east of the building and line up with the doorway by using the parachute at the doorway as a guide. Then as you descend, move forward so you land through the doorway. The advantage to landing here is you can pick up a G43 rifle on this floor. Because there are no stairs or ladders to this floor, the only way you can get to this rifle is by landing on this floor of the building. From here, you can shoot the snipers on the flak tower scaffolding and even the Germans guarding the front of the tower. If you are starting from the ground level, this is a good place to land.

NOTE

This walkthrough begins with landing on the top of the flak tower and working down through the tower to the ground level.

DESTROY THE ARTILLERY GUNS

ROOF

Blockhouse

Rubble
Ramp

Stairs Down to
Upper Gun Level

LEGEND

🔲 Health

Secure Zones

🔲 On the roof

Miscellaneous

← Recommended Path

Weapon Loadout

- Browning Automatic Rifle
  or StG.44

- Mauser

- M1903 Springfield or G43
  (if you have the scope upgrade)

The best place to
land to begin the
mission is on the
roof at the SZ.
Not only does this
provide crates of
ammo and health
kits, but it is also
safe—compared to
the rest of the roof.
The only threat is
a Panzergrenadier
with a Panzerschreck to the north. Quickly take cover
behind a short wall of concrete and, after he fires a rocket,
pop up and kill the enemy.

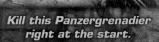

*Kill this Panzergrenadier
right at the start.*

UPPER GUN LEVEL

Antiair Gun

Stairs to Roof

Antiair Gun

Antiair Gun

Stairs to Lower Gun Level

Join up with your allies, engage the enemy to the north, and then advance on the blockhouse.

Other paratroopers have also landed on the roof of the ~~fl~~ak tower and are engaging more Germans. The enemy is ~~c~~oncentrated around the blockhouse at the roof's northern ~~e~~nd. Use your automatic rifle or sniper rifle to clear them ~~ou~~t. A couple of Panzergrenadiers are the main threat, so ~~fo~~cus first on them. Be sure to stay behind cover. As you ~~ru~~n out of targets in your current position, locate another ~~pie~~ce of cover and sprint for it. Engage any new enemies you ~~ca~~n see from this position. Don't rush ahead of your allies

and use caution near the blockhouse. Approach the back of it from the left since enemy reinforcements may come at you from the stairs on the eastern side of the roof.

TIP

The artillery guns that you see poking up through holes in the roof can be destroyed using Gammon grenades. You begin with three and can find more in the crates by the SZ on the lower gun level. Cook off these grenades for about four seconds so you can also kill enemies near the guns before they can run away. This gives you good kill points and pushes you toward an upgrade so you can carry more of these powerful grenades.

Advance down these stairs.

Cover is important if you want to survive this area.

The fighting around the artillery guns is intense.

Descend the stairs to the upper gun level. As you enter this area, be ready for lots of enemies. Grenades work well in here because there is plenty of cover. Concentrate on clearing out the areas around the artillery guns. Start with the one on your right. This prevents enemies from getting in behind you while you are advancing through the rest of this area. Once it is clear, quickly plant a charge on the gun and advance to the next artillery gun.

Be sure to stay behind cover as much as possible during the firefights. These enemies can really hurt you if you are out in the open. When the area around the second gun is secure, blow the gun and use the same tactics to advance and destroy the third (and final) gun. When all three are destroyed, you have one less objective to complete. Go down the stairs near the third artillery gun to get to the lower gun level.

Plant charges on the artillery to destroy them.

DESTROY THE AA GUNS

LOWER GUN LEVEL

Antiair Gun

Side Entrance to Center Room

Side Tunnel

Antiair Gun

Front Entrance to Center Room

Antiair Gun

Stairs to Upper Level Gun

Explosives

Antiair Gun

LEGEND

⊞ **Health**

Secure Zones

[2] On the outside of the lower gun level

Miscellaneous

← Recommended Path

Weapon Loadout

- Browning Automatic Rifle or StG.44
- Mauser

- M1903 Springfield or G43 (if you have the scope upgrade)

This is where the fight gets a bit tougher. As you get to the bottom of the stairs you have a choice—go after the AA guns on the outside of the lower gun level, or clear out the center room. It does not matter which you do first. However, if you clear out the center room first, you can always retreat back into it for health and cover.

Advance into the center room.

Center Room

Stairs Down to
Upper Lift

Side Exit to
Lower Gun Level

Main Exit to
Lower Gun Level

LEGEND

🏥 Health

Miscellaneous

← Recommended Path

Weapon Loadout

- Browning Automatic Rifle or StG.44
- Mauser
- M1903 Springfield or G43 (if you have the scope upgrade)

Resupply here.

Kill the enemies on the catwalk.

As you exit the center room and head out onto the lower gun level, stop by the SZ to replenish your ammo, grenades, and health at the crates. You must now advance around this outer ring and destroy the four AA guns here. Once again, you face plenty of enemies, including several Nazi Storm Elites. Use the crates and other forms of cover as you advance. As you approach that first AA gun, watch the catwalk above it. Enemies like to fire down on you from that position.

Pull back when you see the Nazi Storm Elite coming toward you.

Use your sniper rifle as much as possible to engage the enemy at long range. However, the Germans tend to try to close on your position, so be ready to switch to your automatic rifle. Also, as you get close to an AA gun, throw a grenade at the gun position to kill the enemies next to it. Be sure to cook these grenades so you can kill the enemies before they run away.

An automatic rifle is necessary for groups of enemies charging against you. Mow them down.

Enter the center room from the damaged opening on the western side. Take cover because many enemies are inside here—including a Nazi Storm Elite. Work your way around the outside of the room in a counter-

Clear out the Germans as you work your way around.

clockwise direction. Pay attention to your compass, as the enemies like to hide around corners to ambush you. The Nazi Storm Elite advances slowly toward you. Use grenades to cause him some damage if you need to withdraw. However, the BAR does a good job of taking him out with short bursts aimed at his head. Continue all the way around to the opening where you entered this area.

TIP

Gammon grenades are great for throwing into AA gun positions. Not only do they kill the Germans taking cover there, they also destroy the AA gun at the same time.

Throw grenades from the catwalk into the AA position.

When you run into several Nazi Storm Elites near the third and fourth AA guns, begin to withdraw as far away as possible so that you still have a line of fire to these enemies. Use your sniper rifle to take headshots on them. Or, if several are

Take cover and fire short bursts at the Nazi Storm Elites.

together, throw a Gammon grenade. Although it probably does not kill them, it causes them a lot of damage and makes them easier to finish off. Eliminate the enemies along this area, then blow up any remaining AA guns to complete this objective.

Keep advancing. The third catwalk has stairs on both sides, allowing you to climb up and gain a height advantage that is useful for lobbing grenades or firing on enemies hiding behind cover. You can also use the side tunnel near the second AA gun for cover as well as to try to flank the enemy. While your allies stay on the outside, move around through the tunnel. The tunnel also offers complete cover against gunfire from the enemies on the catwalks.

TIP

Use up all your grenades as you move around the lower gun level. Climb up the stairs to the last catwalk and follow it to the end. Around the corner is a crate of explosives that restocks your grenades.

DISABLE 4TH FLOOR AMMUNITION LIFT CONTROLS

UPPER LIFT

Stairs to
Center Room

Lift to
Upper Shaft

UPPER SHAFT

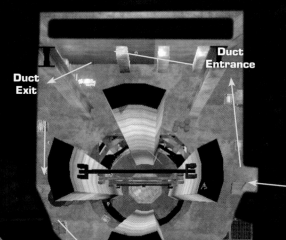

Duct Entrance

Duct Exit

Lift to Upper Lift

Ammo Control Room

Stairs Down to Middle Shaft

Exit to Scaffolding

LEGEND

 Health

Miscellaneous

← Recommended Path

Weapon Loadout

- Browning Automatic Rifle or StG.44
- Mauser

- M1903 Springfield or G43 (if you have the scope upgrade)

These stairs take you down to the upper lift.

It is now time to move down into the belly of the beast. Return to the center room. It should be clear if you already assaulted it. However, it is wise to be cautious in case Germans from the lower gun level retreated into

Activate the lift to go down to the next level.

here during the fighting. Continue to the room's center and descend the stairs to the upper lift. Use caution because a Nazi Storm Elite is waiting for you down there. Make your way around to the lift. Activate the call button to bring the lift up to your level. When it arrives, walk onto it and activate the controls to send it down to the upper shaft level.

Germans are waiting at the bottom for you.

As you are descending on the lift, take cover behind the crates so you are ready for a fight when you get to the bottom. You are now headed toward the ammo control room, so make your assault to the right. Again, use grenades to get those enemies hiding behind cover. Allies join up with you from the left as they enter from the scaffolding.

TIP

When getting off the lift, move to your immediate right. Jump up on some crates to find an opening in the wall. You can climb in this, and then move through a duct. Use melee attacks to knock out vents and you have a perfect spot from which to hit the Germans on their flanks and support your allies. You can exit out the opposite end.

Take these stairs up to the ammo control room.

At the end of this area, you come upon some stairs. Take them up to the top floor of the ammo control room. You must fight more Germans when you get to the top. Watch out for a Panzer-grenadier firing rockets. The windows to the control room are open, so lob some grenades through to kill some of the enemies inside. Advance into the

Throw grenades though the windows.

control room and mop up any remaining enemies. The controls are near the window. Shoot the controls or hit them with melee attacks to disable one of the ammo lifts.

TIP

Before leaving the control room, go down a ladder in the rear of the room. It takes you to a platform with another ladder leading down. Descend to a secret cache of crates of ammo, health, and explosives, as well as a recoilless rifle and StG.44. If you look out the window of this room, you can snipe at enemies below on the lower shaft level. The more you kill from here, the fewer you have to kill when you get down there. Try to get rid of the Nazi Storm Elites if possible. Use the recoilless rifle for this job. Just be sure to swap back before you leave so you have an automatic rifle and a sniper rifle. This room is also accessible through one of the skill drop openings.

After completing the objective, exit the ammo control room and move down to the central walkway. Backtrack to the lift, then continue past it to stairs that take you down the lower shaft.

DISABLE 2ND FLOOR AMMUNITION LIFT CONTROLS

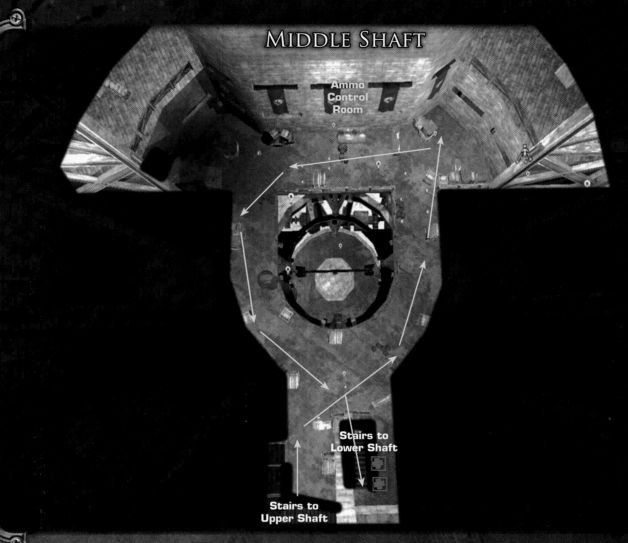

MIDDLE SHAFT

Ammo
Control
Room

Stairs to
Lower Shaft

Stairs to
Upper Shaft

LEGEND

⊞ Health

Miscellaneous

← Recommended Path

Weapon Loadout

- Browning Automatic Rifle
  or StG.44
- Mauser

- M1903 Springfield or G43
  (if you have the scope upgrade)

About halfway down the stairs, take cover behind a large vertical concrete support. Peek around it to shoot at enemies below with your sniper rifle—especially the Nazi Storm Elites. Eliminate all you can from this position, then continue down to the floor of the middle shaft level. Take cover, then clear out the enemies in this area in a counterclockwise direction as you go. Go down the stairs (near the stairs leading up) to the lower shaft level.

Shoot while the Nazi Storm Elite is reloading.

Watch out for enemies shooting through the windows of the control room. Kill them with your sniper rifle.

LOWER SHAFT

Ammo Control Room

Lift Down to Ground Level

Stairs to Middle Shaft

Exit to Scaffolding

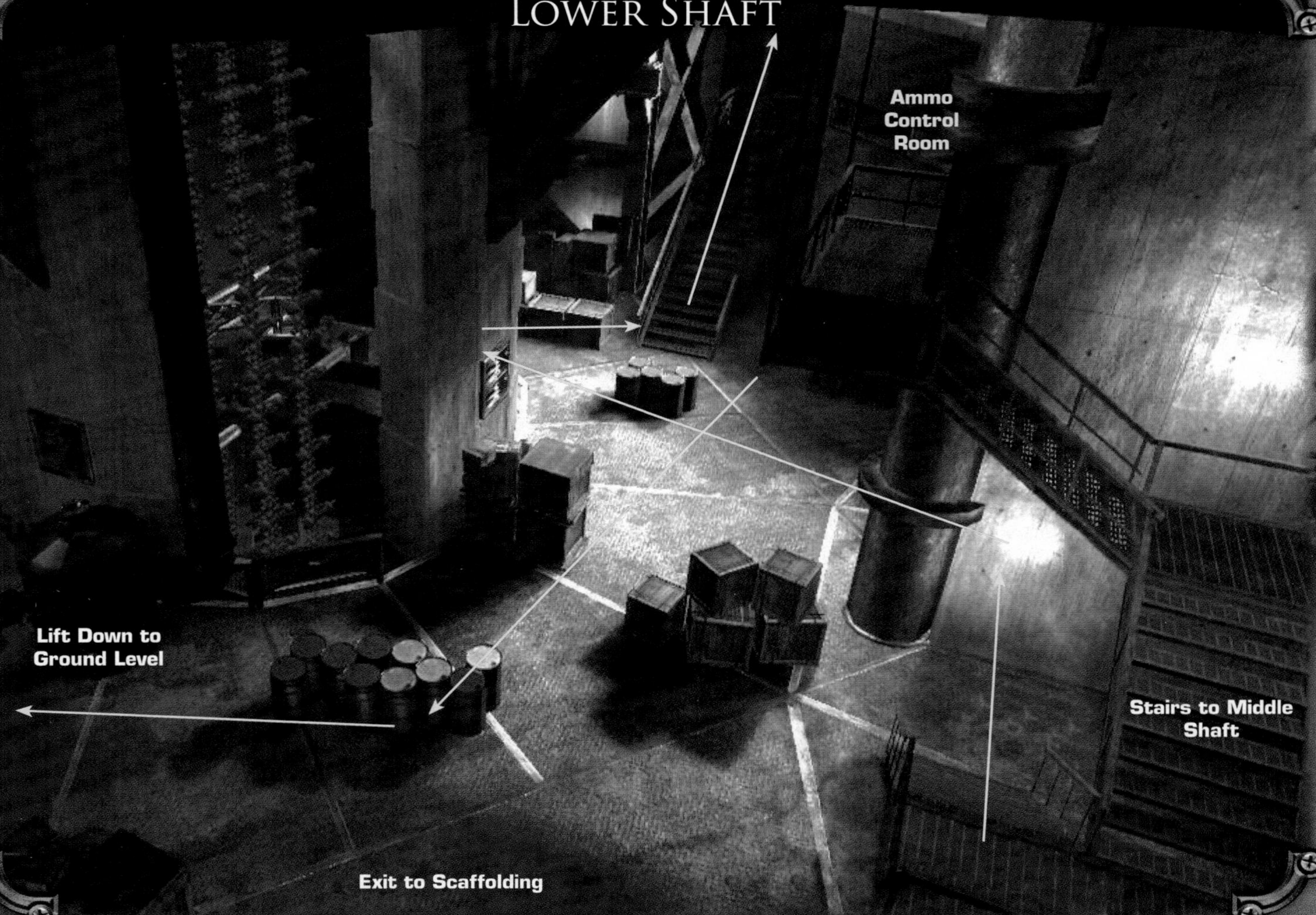

Sprint for these crates, then take cover behind them as you gun down the enemies coming out of the control room.

These stairs do not offer much cover, so get down to the bottom as quickly as you can. Take cover and begin firing at enemies coming at you from the direction of the ammo control room. When the floor is clear, sprint ahead and past the stairs leading up to the control room, taking cover behind some crates. A Nazi Storm Elite comes out, and you want as much cover as possible. As before, wait until he stops to reload, then open up with your automatic rifle. Lots of Germans come pouring out of the ammo control room, so keep up your fire. Your allies hit them from the other side of the stairs, so the Germans find themselves in a deadly crossfire.

Smash this box to disable the ammo lift.

When it finally looks clear, head up the stairs to the ammo control room. Peek around the corner of the door to make sure it is clear, or wait for your allies to enter and do this for you. Move in and disable the controls near the windows. Another objective is completed. Exit the room and move across the lower shaft level to the lift that will take you to the ground level.

TIP

Step out onto the scaffolding and shoot the snipers on other levels of scaffolding. Start sniping at the Germans on the ground outside the flak tower. This may allow your allies on the ground to advance on the flak tower to help you later on.

MECHANICAL ROOM

Lift Between Lower Shaft and Ground Level

Kill this elite while descending on the lift.

Activate the call button to bring the lift up. When it arrives, step onto the platform and use the controls to make it descend. As you go past the mechanical room, watch out for a Nazi Storm Elite. The lift does not stop, but this enemy fires on you. Take cover behind the crates and lob a Gammon grenade. Finish him off with either another Gammon grenade or rifle fire. You will have to come up on this lift later and you don't want to have to worry about this threat again.

ELIMINATE THE ENEMIES ON THE HALFTRACKS

INTERIOR GROUND FLOOR

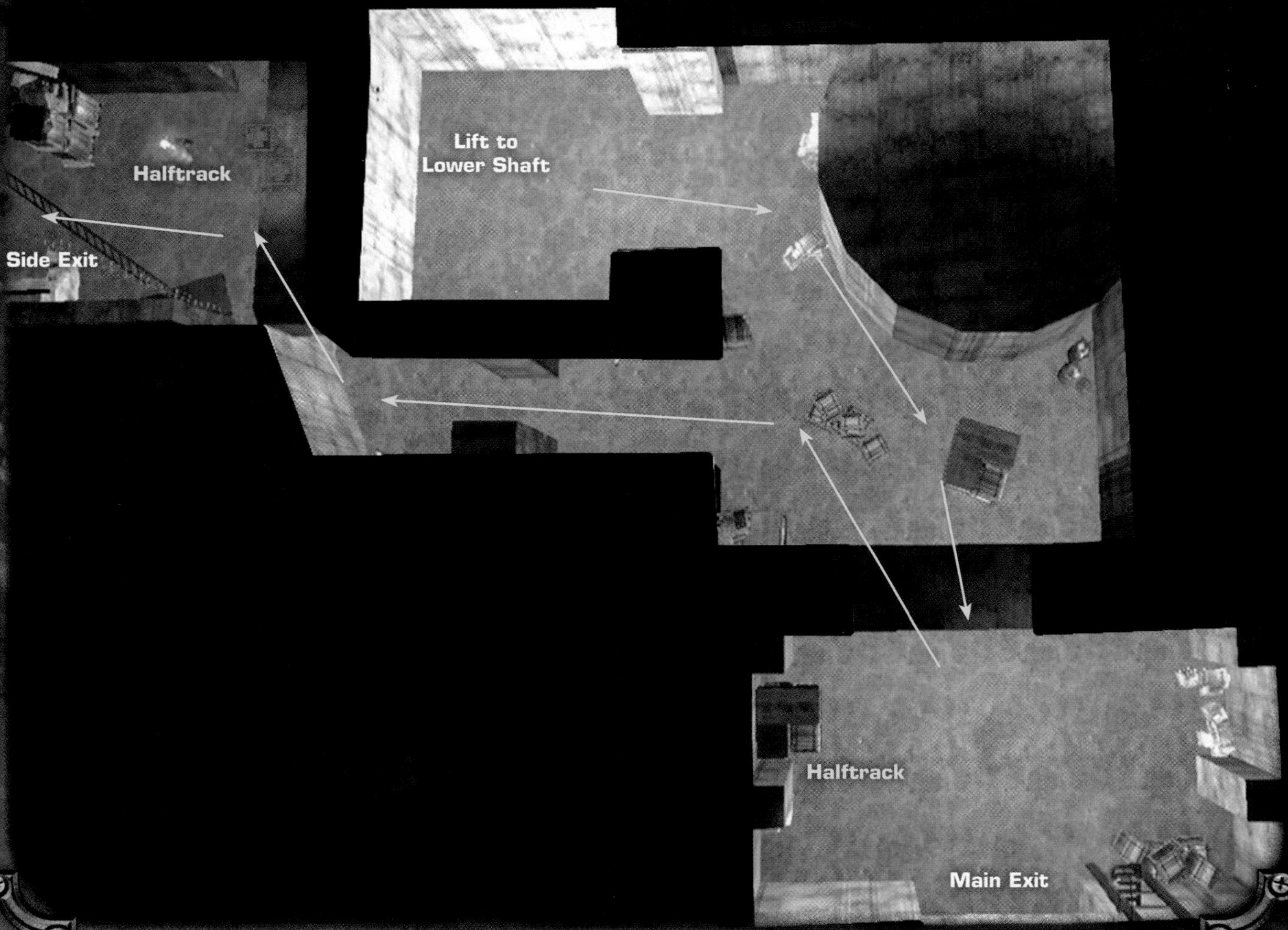

Halftrack

Side Exit

Lift to
Lower Shaft

Halftrack

Main Exit

LEGEND

[■] Health

Miscellaneous

← Recommended Path

Weapon Loadout

- Browning Automatic Rifle
  or StG.44
- M1903 Springfield or G43
  (if you have the scope upgrade)
- Mauser

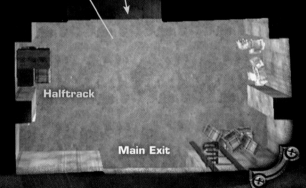

SCAFFOLDING

Entrance to Upper Shaft

Entrance to Lower Shaft

TIP

You can actually use the scaffolding and ladders on the outside of the flak tower to get all the way from the ground level to the lower and upper shaft levels.

LEGEND

Machine Gun Positions

Secure Zones
In courtyard on ground level

Miscellaneous
← Recommended Path

Ladder

Weapon Loadout

- Browning Automatic Rifle or StG.44
- M1903 Springfield or G43 (if you have the scope upgrade)
- Mauser

EXTERIOR GROUND FLOOR

Side Entrance

Halftrack

Main Entrance

Cache

Panzerschreck   Cache   G-13

Recoilless
Rifle

Attacking the halftracks from the rear
is safer because the gunner cannot
turn the gun to shoot you.

When the lift arrives at ground level, step off and move toward the main exit out of the flak tower. Be ready to engage enemies as you advance. Keep pushing until you come to the halftrack from behind. Shoot the gunner to complete one of the objectives. Instead of exiting the tower at this time, go in and continue on to the side exit where you find a second halftrack. Kill the gunner and then exit the tower.

Advance to the left, moving from cover to cover as you engage Germans outside the flak tower. Continue to the last halftrack and kill the gunner. This completes the last of the initial objectives. Continue to clear out any remaining Germans near the entrance before going back inside.

Watch for snipers up high as you move
around at ground level.

Two caches of supplies are in the buildings outside the flak tower near the SZ. You can also find a Panzerschrek near the bottom of the stairs in the northern building, and a recoilless rifle upstairs in the same building.

It's time to go inside.

ASSEMBLE AT MAIN CONTROL ROOM (3RD FLOOR)

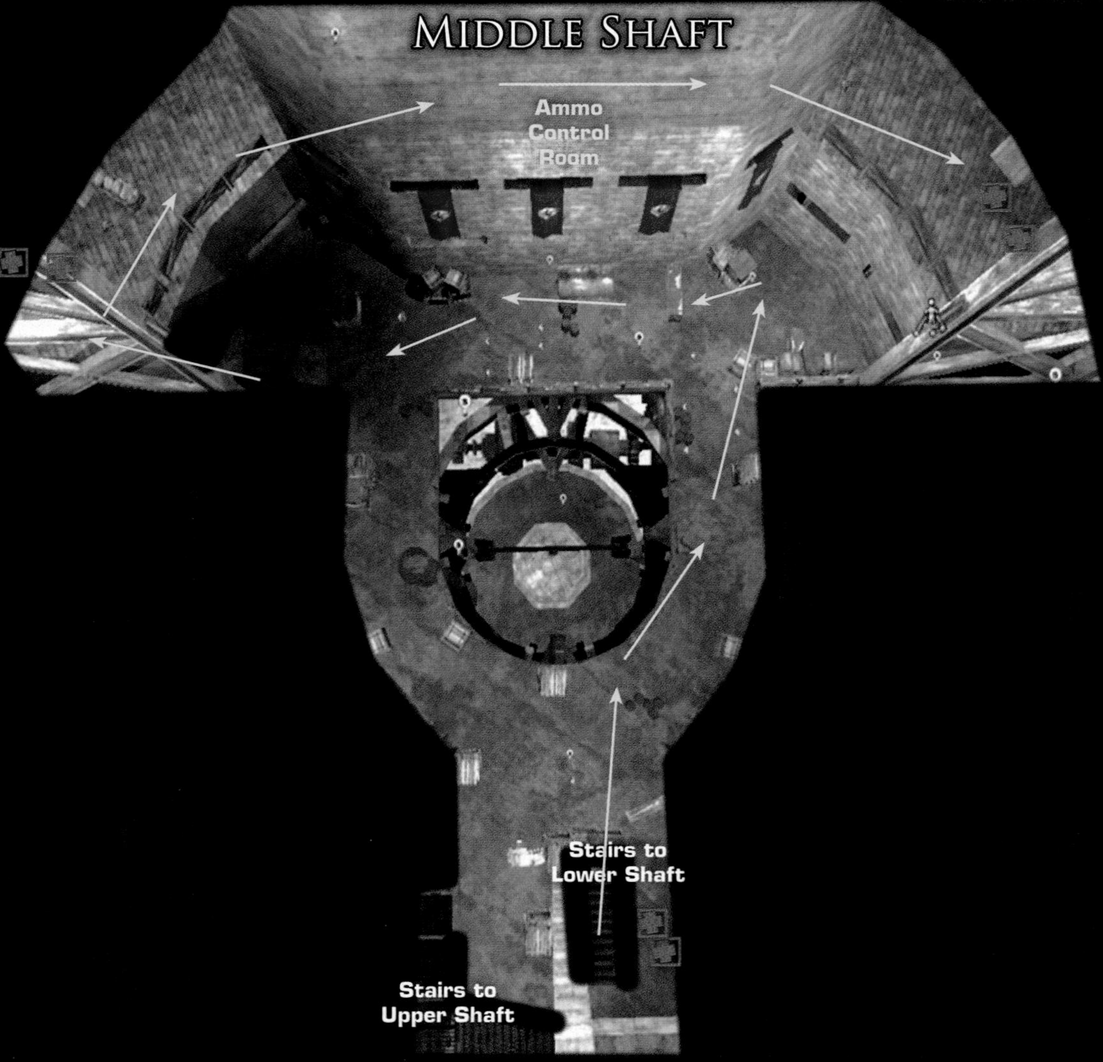

MIDDLE SHAFT

Ammo Control Room

Stairs to Lower Shaft

Stairs to Upper Shaft

Look through the control room windows as you approach the door to see if there are any remaining enemies. You can then shoot right through the window to kill them.

Now that you have secured the flak tower, it is time to head back inside to finish the job. Take the lift back up to the lower shaft level, then continue up the stairs to the middle shaft level. You must face a lot of German defenders

There is a lot more close combat on the middle shaft level.

on your way to the main control room. Assault to the right, watching for enemies firing at you from behind crates as well as through the open windows of the control room.

Continue to the crates below the control room on the right side. From here, engage enemies coming down the stairs from the control room while your allies hit them from the opposite side. Some Nazi Storm Elites are inside, so wait until they come out and shoot them from a distance. When it looks clear, go up the stairs and enter the control room. Use grenades to mop up any remaining enemies if necessary.

TIP

If you are good at throwing grenades at a distance, you can send them flying right through the windows of the control room to kill the enemies inside.

Pass through this room to get to a ladder leading up to your objective.

Advance through the control room to a ladder. Climb it and then advance toward a doorway leading into a conference room. A Nazi Storm Elite is waiting for you inside. Crouch down to one side of the door and peek in to get him to start shooting. When he pauses, peek again and fire quick bursts before ducking back behind cover. Repeat this until the enemy is dead. Usually, other enemies lurk inside as well, so throw in some grenades before moving in to finish them off. Grab some health kits inside here if you need them.

From these crates you can easily fire on enemies coming down the stairs from the control room.

Clear out the conference room while peeking around the door.

ASSEMBLE WITH ENGINEERS IN AMMUNITION STORAGE

AMMO STORAGE

Escape
Tunnel

Cache

Cache

Shotgun

Elevator from
Control Room

LEGEND

🞢 Health

Miscellaneous

← Recommended Path

Weapon Loadout

- Browning Automatic Rifle or StG.44
- Mauser
- M1903 Springfield or G43 (if you have the scope upgrade)

The engineers are ready to blow this tower.

This lift takes you down to your next objective.

When the conference room is clear, enter the small lift that opens up and ride it down to the ammunition storage area. The engineers are down there setting demolitions charges. By the time you meet up with them, this objective is complete.

ESCAPE THE FLAK TOWER

Eliminate these enemies so you can get out without being shot in the back.

Follow the wire out.

As the engineers bug out, some Germans arrive. You must now get out of the flak tower. One of the enemy is a Nazi Storm Elite. Take cover behind one of the steel supports and hammer him with short bursts.

Go back down the stairs and advance to the north, following the demolitions wire into another area. The catwalk ends, so quickly get down into the concrete passageway before enemies shoot you.

Pick up a shotgun and some ammo.

One Nazi Storm Elite down.

Make your way to the stairs at the southern end of this area and follow them out to an area with a crate of weapon ammo, some Gammon grenades, and a shotgun. Swap out your sniper rifle for this close-range weapon because that is the type of combat you will be engaged in next.

This lower area is very dangerous. Steam leaking from pipes has reduced the visibility here. Several Nazi Storm Elites threaten here. They are pretty smart about running away from grenades, so you must carefully cook your Gammon grenades before throwing them. Also, use your automatic rifle to finish them off. Other types of soldiers are here as well, so don't totally fixate on the Elites or the others may get you.

Watch for Germans up above.

This elite is hiding in a little alcove in the center. Bounce a Gammon grenade around a corner to blow him up.

In the southwest corner you can find some health kits as well as more weapons ammo. Also look for Gammon grenades on the ground. Your compass is your friend in here, helping you locate threats you can't see through the steam.

Take the sewers to safety.

Withdraw to cover if you have to as the Elites advance on you. However, by this time, you should be proficient at dealing with them. Continue to follow the wire to a ladder that takes you out of this area. Climb the ladder and enter some sewer pipes. Follow them to exit near the buildings outside the flak tower.

DESTROY THE FLAK TOWER

Detonate the explosives to finish the mission.

Now all that remains is to detonate the explosives down in the ammunition storage area. Move forward and pick up the Hellbox. Twist the detonator to ensure that the flak tower will no longer be a threat to the Allies.

Flak Tower Redux

Take out the snipers on the scaffolding.

Use the recoilless rifle to wipe out the machine gun positions.

After you have finished this mission, it is challenging to try it with different tactics. For example, drop to the buildings outside of the flak tower and complete your objectives by fighting your way in. The best place to begin is on the upper floors of the buildings with a sniper rifle. Use it to clear the scaffolding of enemy snipers as well as to clear a way to the entrance for yourself and your allies. Then you basically just go about the objectives in reverse order, starting with the halftracks and ending with the artillery guns. Also, try experimenting with using the scaffolding to get to the various levels from the outside of the flak tower rather than fighting your way through enemies inside.

Use the scaffolding to get from the ground up to higher levels.

MULTIPLAYER

While the single-player campaign missions are awesome and the enemy AI can be extremely challenging, sometimes you want to take the battle in a different direction—play against other gamers. *Medal of Honor Airborne* offers you the chance to do just that.

SETTING UP A GAME

Getting into a game is very easy. From the main menu, select the multi-player option, which varies by platform. For example, if you are playing on the Xbox 360, select Xbox Live. You can then select what type of match you want. A Quick Match puts you in an open game as quickly as possible. If you want to be more selective, Custom Match lets you pick the specifics of a match, and then searches for matches that meet your criteria. You can also use Create Match to host a match with all of your own settings. Let's take a look at the different settings that you can use to customize your game.

MAP

Multiplayer mode lets you choose from six different maps. Three are from the single-player campaign: Husky, Avalanche, and Neptune. The multiplayer games only use part of the single-player maps, creating a small play area for intense combat. The other three maps—Destroyed Village, Remagen, and The Hunt—are taken from previous *Medal of Honor* games and updated for *Medal of Honor Airborne*.

GAME MODE

This is where you can select which type of game you would like to play. Your options are Team Deathmatch, Team Deathmatch Airborne, and Objective Airborne.

ROUNDS

Here you can determine how many rounds make up a match. You can choose from a single round, the best of three, the best of five, and the best of seven.

ROUND TIME

This let's you adjust the amount of time each round lasts. Your choices are 3 minutes, 5 minutes, 10 minutes, 15 minutes, and 20 minutes.

FRIENDLY FIRE

With this option, you can select whether you want friendly fire to cause damage or not. If you select *yes*, then friendly soldiers will take damage from your bullets as well as your grenades.

UPGRADES

For a match, you can select whether weapon upgrades are allowed. You can choose *no* and limit players to only the basic versions of all weapons. If you choose *yes*, then players can earn upgrades for their weapons normally. The final option, *full*, lets all players start out with fully upgraded weapons.

MAX PLAYERS

This option allows you to select the maximum number of players for a match. You can choose from only two players to up to 12 players.

PRIVATE MATCH

If you want only people you invite to play your match, then select *yes* for this option. If you need more people, then select *no* and open up your match to the public.

TYPES OF GAMES

Threre are three different types of games.

TEAM DEATHMATCH

The standard Team Deathmatch puts players into two teams as the Axis and the Allies. Both start at their spawn locations on the map and try to kill each other. The team with the most points when the timer runs out wins.

TEAM DEATHMATCH AIRBORNE

Team Deathmatch Airborne is similar to Team Deathmatch except that the Allies spawn in the air and drop down on to the map. This can be a fun, unique way to play because the Allies can drop down anywhere while the Axis team can try to kill the enemy while they are in the air and cannot fire back.

OBJECTIVE AIRBORNE

The final mode is Objective Airborne. The Axis players spawn on the map while the Allied players drop from the air. Each map has three objectives that must be captured. To capture an objective, move next to the flag and the capturing process begins. The game ends when one team controls all three objectives or the time runs out. The winner is the team with the most points.

WEAPONS LOADOUTS

Before starting a round, select the type of weapon you want to carry. You are limited to those weapons for your side—either Allied or Axis weapons. Unlike the single-player missions, in multiplayer, you can only carry a primary weapon, a pistol, and grenades. Therefore, you must determine what role you want to play during the match. You can choose a different type of primary weapon during a round, however you do not get that new weapon until you die and then respawn.

You can also pick up weapons dropped by dead allies and enemies. This is the only way you can get a weapon that is available only to the opposing team.

EARNING WEAPON UPGRADES

By using a specific weapon to kill enemies, you can earn upgrades for that weapon. Only kills in Ranked Matches count toward upgrades and they are cumulative for your player profile. Therefore, the more you use a weapon, the faster you can upgrade it. The following is a table of the number of kills you need for upgrading weapons.

WEAPON UPGRADES

Weapon	40 Kills—1st Upgrade	Benefit	150 Kills—2nd Upgrade	Benefit	320 Kills—3rd Upgrade	Benefit
M1 Garand	Ported Gas Cylinder & Front Sight	+ Accuracy	Lock Bar Rear Sight	+ Zoom	Grenade Launcher	+ Launch Grenades
K98k	Polished Bolt & Action	+ Rate of Fire	5-Round Stripper Clip	+ Faster Reload	Grenade Launcher	+ Launch Grenades
Thompson	Front Pistol Grip	+ Accuracy	Cutts Compensator	+ Reduced Recoil	50-Round Drum	+ Ammo Capacity

(table continued on next page)

MEDAL OF HONOR AIRBORNE

WEAPON UPGRADES (CONT.)

Weapon	40 Kills—1st Upgrade	Benefit	150 Kills—2nd Upgrade	Benefit	320 Kills—3rd Upgrade	Benefit
MP40	2 Taped Magazines	+ Faster Reload	64-Round Magazine	+ Ammo Capacity	SS Dagger	+ Melee Attack
BAR	Compensator	+ Reduced Recoil	A2 Rear Sight	+ Zoom	2 Taped Magazines	+ Faster Reload
StG.44	Flash Suppressor	+ Reduced Recoil	2 Taped Magazines	+ Faster Reload	ZF4 Scope	+ Zoom
Springfield Sniper Rifle	Polished Bolt & Action	+ Rate of Fire	5-Round Stripper Clip	+ Faster Reload	Grenade Launcher	+ Launch Grenades
G43 (starts with scope)	20-Round Magazine	+ Ammo Capacity	Eye Piece	+ Reduced Recoil	Grenade Launcher	+ Launch Grenades
Recoilless Rifle	Scoped Sight	+ Zoom	Shell Bag	+ Ammo Capacity + 1	Shell bag	+ Ammo Capacity + 1
Panzerschreck	Better Sight	+ Accuracy	Shell Bag	+ Ammo Capacity + 1	Shell bag	+ Ammo Capacity + 1

SCORING AND RANKS

The scoring system is fairly simple. During a round, you earn points for killing enemies, working together as a team, and capturing objectives. Here is a breakdown of points.

SCORING

Action	Points Earned
Kill an enemy	2
Kill assist (hit an enemy who is then killed by a teammate within a short amount of time)	1
Capture an objective	2

SCORING

Action	Points Earned
Be with teammate during objective capture (cumulative with points earned for capturing the objective)	1
Suicide (grenade, rocket, fall)	-2
Team kill	-4

As you play Ranked Matches and earn points, your total score is used to determine your rank. The following is a table of the ranks to which you can be promoted.

MULTIPLAYER RANKS

Rank		Allied Rank		Axis Rank	Points Needed (Ranked Matches only)
1	R	Recruit	R	Recruit	0
2	P	Private	P	Grenadier	30
3	⋀	Private First Class	◆	Obergrenadier	60
4	⋀	Corporal	▽	Obergefreiter	120

MULTIPLAYER RANKS (CONT.)

Rank		Allied Rank		Axis Rank	Points Needed (Ranked Matches only)
5		Sergeant		Unteroffizier	180
6		Staff Sergeant		Unterfeldwebel	240
7		Sergeant First Class		Feldwebel	300
8		Master Sergeant		Oberfeldwebel	400
9		First Sergeant		Stabsfeldwebel	700
10		Second Lieutenant		Leutnant	1,000
11		First Lieutenant		Oberleutnant	1,300
12		Captain		Hauptmann	1,600
13		Major		Major	2,000
14		Lieutenant Colonel		Oberstleutnant	2,400
15		Colonel		Oberst	2,800
16		Brigadier General		Generalmajor	3,200
17		Major General		Generalleutnant	3,700
18		Lieutenant General		Generaloberst	4,100
19		General		General	4,500
20		General of the Army		Generalfeldmarshall	4,900

MULTIPLAYER TACTICS

LANDING

The Allies drop in on the map for two of the three types of multiplayer games. While falling, you have a great view of the map below and can see the enemies running around like ants. Use this advantage to land behind them or somewhere with cover. You can also drop right on any of the objectives as well as rooftops. Just be careful when dropping next to enemies since they may shoot you before you can even hit the ground. Do not forget to use the deadly melee kick attack as you land right on top of an enemy.

In multiplayer games, every landing is a greased landing. Therefore, when playing as the Allies in a game with a drop, you can try to land anywhere without worrying about botching the landing. When playing as an Axis soldier, attack the paratrooper as soon as he touches down because he will be ready to fight.

Look Up

The biggest difference between *Medal of Honor Airborne* and other multiplayer games is the drop. When playing as the Axis, you have to train yourself to look not only left and right, but also up so the enemy does not surprise you. The paratroopers are targets while they are in the air. Use an automatic rifle or other high-powered weapon to kill them in midair when they can't shoot back.

TIP

If you are good with grenades, cook one off so that it detonates in midair right next to a dropping paratrooper. Not only is this cool, but it also earns you an achievement.

Use the Heights

All the multiplayer maps have heights, so use them. Verticality is a key part of this game, and the more you use it, the better you do. As a paratrooper, you can drop onto rooftops and then fire down on enemies below. However, most heights can be reached from the ground, such as by ladders, for example, so Axis players should also use the heights—especially since Allies expect to find you running around on the ground.

Play as a Team

Teamwork is so important. All three types of games are team-based. Communicate with the other people on your team, letting them know what you are doing and where you going. In the Objective Airborne game, keep at least one player back to guard the flags you have captured. Stay off to one side so you have cover and a clear field of fire at the area around the flag. Since the game is over when one team captures all three positions, you don't want to have to recapture the same flags again and again.

TIP

Use grenades a lot. The more kills you get with them, the more upgrades your earn—each of which allows you to carry more grenades at one time. You always start out with grenades no matter what weapon you select. Just be sure to cook grenades before throwing since you don't want the enemy to kick them back at you. Being killed by your own grenade is so embarrassing.

The Right Weapon

The weapon you carry really determines the way you play a multiplayer game. Since you can only have one weapon in addition to your pistol, your options are somewhat limited. You are a sniper, a close-range assaulter, or a medium-range gunner.

TIP

If you take a Panzerfaust or recoilless rifle, you can only fire it when in scope view. Therefore, find a safe position with some protection that allows you to take your time with each shot. Have your pistol out when running around the map since you can fire it quickly for defense.

THE MAPS

HUSKY

LEGEND

Objectives

This map is the central part of the town. You can enter the market buildings, using them not only to get from one point to another, but also for defending the flags below.

Use the rooftops to kill enemies down below.

The flags are all out in the open, so after capturing one, find cover from which to defend it.

The city wall provides a good way to get around and a position on the map's edge from which to shoot at your enemies.

AVALANCHE

LEGEND

Objectives

This map features the amphitheatre as well as the central area. Use the many ruins for cover as well as the aqueducts for a height advantage.

You can drop down anywhere in the ruins.

Use the aqueducts and the upper levels of the amphitheatre for sniping at enemies.

A couple of the objectives are located near the edges of the map.

NEPTUNE

This map is a bit different than the single-player version. You are only on the western side centered on the approach to the radar bunker. Each team spawns with a base—the Axis in the bunker to the north and the Allies near the house in the south. In addition to the open terrain between the two bases, there is also a tunnel running beneath the central area that leads right into the bunker.

The bunker and the house serve as bases.

The pillbox also has an entrance down into the tunnel.

There are entrances to the tunnels from inside the bunker as well as through an opening just north of the house.

DESTROYED VILLAGE

LEGEND

Objective

This map consists of a central group of buildings, buildings on the perimeter, and a street running between the two. There are many rooftops and some have hole through which paratroopers can drop right into cover. Some long sight lines make this a good map for those who like to snipe.

This is a fun map to drop into.

As the Axis, look for ways to get up to the rooftops.

The central objective is located on the second floor of this bombed-out house. You can take this ramp of lumber up to the location or use a ladder right under the flag.

THE HUNT

LEGEND

Objectives

This map is dominated by a church and graveyard on one side and a village on the other. There are good heights to use as well as many buildings to move through while under cover. A good tactic is to cross the roads at a sprint so enemy snipers have less of a chance of shooting you.

A lot of the rooftops are damaged, allowing paratrooper to drop through to interior rooms.

The church dominates one corner of the map and is near one of the objectives.

Both of the other flags can be easily defended while taking cover in nearby buildings.

REMAGEN

LEGEND
Objectives

Remagen is another city map. However, this one has narrow streets with buildings that seem to tower over them. The central house is one building, offering a lot of interior close combat. The clock tower is a sniper's dream, but can be accessed from the ground as well as the rooftops. This maps combines a lot of close-range combat with long-range sniping.

Dropping into Remagen offers many places to land at various elevations.

This walled walkway offers cover along the sides, allowing you to get through an area quickly and safely.

The clock tower usually has a sniper in it. If you are on the ground, be careful. However, if you are on top, watch out for other snipers trying to knock you off your perch.

The central house offers room-to-room fighting. You can also access the roof from the balcony overlooking the Axis headquarters.

AWARDS

Medal of Honor Airborne offers a number of different awards that you can earn.

STARS

After completing each mission, you are awarded a number of stars based on your performance. The star rating is determined by the number of points you score according to the following formula:

(weapons accuracy percentage) x 100 + number of kills - (number of player deaths) x 10 = Points

Star Rating	Points Required
1 Star	0
2 Stars	40
3 Stars	80
4 Stars	135
5 Stars	150

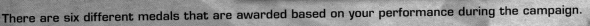
MEDALS

There are six different medals that are awarded based on your performance during the campaign.

SOLDIER MEDAL

Awarded for exceptionally meritorious service in a position of great responsibility.

REQUIREMENT: Equip and use all weapons in the game.

BRONZE STAR

Awarded to Army personnel who distinguish themselves by heroic or meritorious service in connection with military operations.

REQUIREMENT: Earn a 5-star rating on all missions in the Easy difficulty.

LEGION OF MERIT

Awarded to Army personnel for exceptionally meritorious conduct in the performance of outstanding services.

REQUIREMENT: Complete any mission without dying.

SILVER STAR

Awarded to Army personnel for gallantry in action while serving in any capacity.

REQUIREMENT: Earn a 4-star rating on all missions in the Medium difficulty.

WORLD WAR II VICTORY MEDAL

Awarded to Army personnel for one year of honorable federal military service during the war.

REQUIREMENT: Complete all missions.

DISTINGUISHED SERVICE CROSS

Awarded to Army personnel for acts of heroism that do not warrant the Medal of Honor.

REQUIREMENT: Earn a 3-star rating on all missions in the Hard difficulty.

AWARDS

XBOX 360 ACHIEVEMENTS

SINGLE-PLAYER ACHIEVEMENTS

	Achievement Name	Description	Gamerscore Reward
	Jump Training	Completed jump training	5
	Go Go Go!	Got pushed out of the plane	5
	Greased Landing	Touched down with a greased landing	5
	Flared Landing	Touched down with a flared landing	5
	Death from Above	Killed an enemy with a melee kick	10
	Jumpmaster	Discovered one skill drop location in each mission	25
	Master Parachutist	Discovered all skill drop locations in the game	40
	Crack Shot	Got 10 headshots in a row	25
	Tick-tick-BOOM!	Killed three enemies with a cooked grenade	20
	5-in-a-Row!	Earned a 5-in-a-row	20
	Homerun!	Killed an enemy using sprint melee	10
	Shoot to Kill	Killed an enemy while moving in ironsights	10
	In Yer Face!	Killed an enemy by kicking a grenade at him	20
	Purple Heart	Recovered full health after being on verge of death state	10
	Pop-n-Drop	Crouch sprinted between cover objects	5
	Weapon Handler	Fully upgraded one weapon	25
	Weapon Specialist	Fully upgraded five weapons	50

Achievement Name	Description	Gamerscore Reward
Weapon Master	Fully upgraded all weapons	75
Cheat Death	Completed an operation without dying	20
Village of Adanti	Completed Operation Husky	15
Paestum Ruins	Completed Operation Avalanche	20
D-Day in Reverse	Completed Operation Neptune	25
Nijmegan Bridge	Completed Operation Market Garden	30
War Machine	Completed Operation Varsity	35
Der Flakturm	Completed Der Flakturm	40
Complete on Casual	Completed the game on Easy difficulty	25
Complete on Normal	Completed the game on Normal difficulty	50
Complete on Expert	Completed the game on Expert difficulty	75
	Total	700

MULTIPLAYER ACHIEVEMENTS

Achievement Name	Description	Gamerscore Reward
MP—Distinguished Service Cross	Got over 1,000 kills and 500 Objective Points in Ranked Matches	75
MP—Distinguished Service Medal	Got over 500 kills and 250 Objective Points in Ranked Matches	25
MP—Silver Star	Got over 100 first place finishes in Ranked Matches	0
MP—Legion of Merit	Got over 30 Objective Points in a Ranked Match	20
MP—Soldier's Medal	Got 20 kill assists throughout a career in Ranked Matches	20

	Achievement Name	Description	Gamerscore Reward
	MP—Bronze Star	Got over 20 top three finishes in Ranked Matches	0
	MP—Purple Heart	Recovered full health after being on verge of death state	10
	MP—World War II Victory Medal	Came in first place on every map in any game mode in Ranked Matches	0
	MP—American Campaign Medal	Was on the winning team for every map in Ranked Matches	0
	MP—EAM Campaign Medal	Played every map at least once in a Ranked Match	25
	MP—Good Conduct Medal	Played 20 consecutive Ranked Matches without getting a team kill	0
	MP—Presidential Unit Citation	Got 20 Team Points in a Ranked Match	30
	MP—Meritorious Unit Citation	Got 10 Team Points in a Ranked Match	20
	MP—Paratrooper's Badge	Killed an enemy with a melee kick	10
	MP—Combat Infantryman Badge	Killed an enemy player while he was parachuting	10
	MP—Pistol Whip	Killed an enemy with a pistol melee attack	10
	MP—Human Flak Gun	Killed an enemy player with a grenade while he was parachuting	5
	MP—Weapon Virtuoso	Upgraded all weapons in Ranked Matches	40
		Total	300

DEVELOPER INTERVIEWS

While writing this book, I had the opportunity to travel to the Electronic Arts Los Angeles campus and talk to several of the people who created *Medal of Honor Airborne*. Through these interviews, I was able to get a much better understanding of not only the best ways to play the game, but also all the hard work that went into creating the game. I want to thank Bryce Yang at EA Los Angeles for setting up this visit and these interviews and for all the extra help he provided for this guide. I have included excerpts from these interviews with several different people who were instrumental in bringing *Medal of Honor Airborne* to fruition.

PATRICK GILMORE—EXECUTIVE PRODUCER AND VP

MK: What previous projects have you worked on?

PG: I was the executive producer on the first *Medal of Honor*.

MK: What was the idea behind *MOH Airborne*?

PG: To take the franchise to the next generation. *MOH* has always been about the big moments of WWII and the men who were caught up in this spectacular stuff. But with *Airborne*, we wanted to get the focus back on the people and back on the singular experience of the war. Our way of doing that was to pick a specific division of the armed forces and focus on that singular experience. And the experience we went after was the Airborne. The only thing we could think of that would be more intense than being on a Higgins boat on Utah Beach when the ramp goes down would be being in a C-47 flying over Utah Beach, jumping into midair all by yourself, and then falling behind enemy lines. Each of those are defining moments when you can be a hero. The whole game is based on that one core concept—the first step is everything. The experience that follows is designed to follow on that one key moment of choice.

MK: How long have you been working on *MOHA*?

PG: About two and a half years. We started toward the end of *European Assault* and built a bunch of prototypes in the *Pacific Assault* engine.

MK: How many people are involved in making *Airborne*?

PG: From start to finish, about 110 have worked on some part of it.

MK: What are your goals for the project and some of the challenges?

PG: To make the best *MOH* ever. We wanted to do this through innovation and break the formula from the outset. Previous *MOH* was linear and a lot of first-person shooters are the same way. You walk here, trigger an engagement, fight it, then go on to the next. We wanted to do something different and it was all centered around the jump. You can drop anywhere. That didn't work with the linear-type game. So we had to create a whole new game that would let you go anywhere and would still work.

MK: Do you think this type of design encourages replayability?

PG: Definitely. I have spent more time playing Operation Husky than I have ever spent playing any other whole game. And I'm still not bored of it. I was playing it just yesterday. That mission has stood up for eight months now. We didn't design it for replayability. We designed it to get to a higher level of emotional truth. We wanted to create emotional surprise for the player.

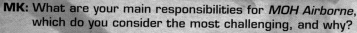
CHRIS BUSSE—PRODUCER

MK: What are your main responsibilities for *MOH Airborne*, which do you consider the most challenging, and why?

CB: Getting all the levels and the content coordinated. All the art assets, the sound assets, the design of the levels—making sure it all comes together.

MK: Are the missions based on actual historical actions?

CB: Absolutely. Each of the operations that we have in the game is an operation that the Airborne actually dropped into. Our specific actions that occur in the game are necessarily actual. The locale, the basic goal of the real-life operation is very similar to what we are doing.

MK: How did the team balance the game's realism and playability?

CB: It is a spectrum and you choose where on that spectrum you want to be. The vast majority of people, I feel, want something that's pretty accurate, that's in the times, and is indicative of what could have happened. We are definitely inspired by the events, but want to make sure that the player is getting an indication of what it would be like to be an airborne soldier in WWII. However, each of the missions has some license we take with reality. That is mostly so we can give the best gameplay experience possible. Dropping into Sicily 30 miles from your DZ and marching through shrubs—I don't know if that is going to be exciting for people. We want to make sure that the action stays high throughout the whole game. Making the game fun all the time is my number one goal. When we took license, it was in order to be fun.

MK: What types of people come together to create a mission?

CB: It is actually a pretty diverse group. Each of our missions has a lead artist and a lead designer. Then they would draw in one to four more designers and one to four more artists. When I say artists, there are modelers, texturers, shader guys, lighters, and then a cinematics department for the part in the plane. The audio department is another five to six people, so each mission is a collaboration of about 25 people.

MK: When designing a level or mission, what is the process? What is the first step, and so forth?

CB: The first thing you do is the story arc. Then within each operation, we had two to three different locales, built them up in two to three maps, stood them up really roughly, and saw how they played. As time went on, we realized that these are the missions that are feeling good and hit our tenets of open space and verticality in the level that we wanted. Then, once we selected our missions, it is really kind of seven stages that we went through. Getting it up on its feet in a basic block form. Then getting it populated. Getting it textured in rough form to then see how it is. Refining the objectives and the fights and getting the layout right. Then lighting comes in at the end. There was a lot of going back to fix little things here and there until we got it right. We worked on our X level—Operation Husky—for quite a while getting everything right. Then, once we had it, we went into full production on the other levels quicker since we had already proven what works and what doesn't. You have to test all your assumptions, listen to what the software is telling you, to make sure you have what you intended.

MK: Is there something you want players to know about the game, that they would not realize for themselves?

CB: The last level of the game is arguably the best level ever in a *Medal of Honor* game. It is just awesome—the verticality, the intensity of the fights, the space that you are in, the action the player encounters. As a final level, it just kind of sums up what the game is all about. It is kind of the final exam. I have played it over 100 times and still love it.

KEN HARSHA—PRODUCTION DESIGNER

MK: What is your background?

KH: My background is in feature film animation story development. I worked on *Shrek*, *Prince of Egypt*, and then with Disney on *Treasure Planet*. I was also the director of concept art and cinematics for *Golden Eye: Rogue Agent* with EA.

MK: What are your main responsibilities for *MOH Airborne*? Which do you consider the most challenging, and why?

KH: I was the producer of pre-production and the production designer. I directed a group of game designers and concept artists as we designed the blueprint for the missions. We researched, whiteboarded, and then pre-visualized every mission in the game. Our thorough pre-production gave production a solid foundation to build on.

MK: Where does research come into play during the design of a game?

KH: In every phase. The game designers come up with an idea for a mission and its objectives. My first goal was to get a deeper understanding each region and its unique history.

We scoured through books, the Internet, videos, and audio files, and talked to experts in an effort to get a solid picture of the history of the area. From that research my concept artists (led by Toby Wilson) begin to digitally construct the layouts for our virtual location designs.

MK: Did you or the team travel to the actual locations for the missions? If so, where?

KH: We did send a team to Europe to photograph many of the historical locations that were going to be representing in the game. In our quest to create exciting environments for gameplay, we broadened our research to areas near the historical sites. Any areas that were regionally correct, and that we thought could add some visual punch to the look of our game, were added to our reference collection as well.

In the end we tried to create sets that were informed by history, looked authentic, and were conducive to really fun multi-tiered game play.

MK: Do you feel the art helps set the tone for a mission?

KH: As the production designer of the game, setting the visual (emotional) tone for *MOHA* was my primary goal. What we set out to do was to revisit/reinvent the look of *MOH*. We wanted to give the player an immediate sense of theme and location for each mission so they could be "in the moment" while they're playing the game. Our goal was to put the player into an authentic and immersive environment that truly allows them to feel what it would be like to jump out of a C47 airplane as it wings its way over a war torn Europe.

MK: What type of research went into the weapons?

KH: The weapons are pretty much a given for this type of game. What we really looked into was the field modifications that the troops might have done on their own. What they might have modified, added onto, or taped onto their guns as a result of their battlefield experience.

MK: Did you also do research on the uniforms and clothing?

KH: We wanted to be authentic with our uniforms in the game. We also needed to push the visual contrast between the uniforms of the Nazis and the Allies. We were influenced by the look of Norman Rockwell paintings for the Allies and by the work of J.C. Leyendecker for the Nazis. With the Allies, we focused on the crumpled, well worn, uniform of the rugged individual. For the Nazis, we went for a more squared off and rigid (machine made) look.

MK: What sources did you use for your information?

KH: We used everything we could get our hands on: Internet, books, movies, audio recordings, WWII history experts, fieldtrips to museums, etc. We also had a guy in Europe that was able to get us some of the harder interior reference material that we were looking for.

One of the most useful books we came across was filled with page after page of Nazi bunker layout illustrations. We used that book heavily for Operation Neptune, and for the Flak tower on our final mission.

In some instances, where we could not find hard facts, we had to improvise a bit. In Flak Tower we had to figure out a way to get all of those huge 128mm shells up to the quad set of dual 128s located on the top of the building. One of my concept artists, Daniel Cheng, found an image of a shell conveyor on line. That conveyor became the centerpiece for the Flak Tower interior and was probably very similar in design to what the Nazis would have used to move those huge 128 shells up to the 80 foot roof top of the tower.

MK: How important is historical accuracy in *MOHA* and how is it balanced with playability?

KH: We looked at the historical events of the war, and tried to give the player an authentic feel for what it would feel like to be in that environment, at that time in history. Some of the locations the player will drop into were tuned to make them better for gameplay—some were more heavily tuned than others.

It's a given that to make good gameplay we had to play fast and loose with some aspects of history, and the topography of a location. We built a city in Italy to represent an airdrop location in operation Husky. The city looks and feels authentic, but if you look it up you won't find it on any map. And yet it "feels" correct. Our focus was to establish authentic aesthetics for the game, and to give the player a memorable, high-quality game experience. We needed to have really dynamic vertical gameplay first and foremost.

MK: What aspect of your work are you proud of?

KH: I am really proud of the immersive visual density and authenticity that we were able to get into the game. I am proud of the work my crew has done on this production and the new game design methodologies we pioneered in the creation of this game. I hope the gamers have as much of a good time playing *MOHA* as we did making it.

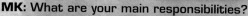

REX DICKSON—LEAD DESIGNER

MK: What are your main responsibilities?

RD: I run the design department. Mostly it is problem solving, like a free safety. You don't own any mission individually, but you are always jumping in to help people get their work done. I am also the liaison with the production side. Producers will come to me and want something, then I will have to figure out how to do it. It is also about communicating the vision of the game—making sure the team understands and is on board with the idea of what we are trying to achieve. A lot of it is also motivation, being a leader, getting people excited about it.

MK: What are your favorite weapons to use during missions?

RD: That is a tough call. I am equally torn between the shotgun and the sniper rifle. I honestly feel like we've made one of the best shotguns that has ever been in a FPS game. It is closely tied in with our kinetic death system—just like the nature of what a shotgun does. The sniper rifle in this game is kind of unique. Because the game is sandbox-oriented, there are places you can get on top of and just try to snipe out the entire level. This game has a unique sniper experience. Most games when you are in a sniper level, you know you are in a sniper level. It is very forced and staged. In our game, there are sniper opportunities everywhere. You can almost deplete an entire level of enemies by just staying up on the rooftops.

MK: Can you share some secrets about the game?

RD: You get the more out of the game, the more creative you are. Completely free yourself from the linear design where you are strung along and open your mind. The game will start rewarding you as you do this.

MK: Do you have a suggestion for a player new to the *MOH* series that will help them be a better player?

RD: If you are just starting the game, land near the green smoke grenades, just to get your bearings first. You land with your allies and they are there to help protect you. It is usually safe to land there. Other strategies are always look for flanks. Every fight has a way to get around something. Move up with your allies and while they are engaging the enemy, get around behind them. It really rewards you when you start looking for those things. If you are low on health, head to a green smoke grenade and a health crate will restore all your health. If you are new to *MOH*, then experiment with peek and lean and the crouch sprint. You really have to use cover. If you try to run and gun, you are going to die a lot. Getting the timing right on cooked grenades is another really big thing in the game. Experiment with it to get it right.

MK: How important are rooftops and heights in this game?

RD: It depends on your style of play. There are a lot of advantages. However, there is not a lot of cover and no ammo to pick up. If there is a street fight and you are the one guy picking off the enemy from above, rooftops can be pretty powerful. The only level that does not really have a lot of heights is Operation Neptune.

MK: What is the greatest hurdle you had to overcome when making a game of this type?

RD: The two biggest hurdles were the Affordance AI—working with the procedural AI system. The other one was nonlinear level design.

In the first one, when you move to a procedural system, you are doing something different. The way we have always done things up to this point, especially FPS games, is the player walks up to a trigger and then it sends an AI to this cover, this AI over to this position. The designer had specific control over exactly who went where and everything. You were completely in control of the set. Procedural AI took all of that control out of our hands. All we could do is spawn these guys in, give them an idea of where the fight we want them in was, and put some cover in. And then they just think for themselves.

For the nonlinear level, the challenge was getting it to work. When we started it was too open and the player could stay out of the engagement area, and just pick off enemies. So what we did was scrunch everything in closer, so the player had to get more involved instead of just staying back all the time. Also, we used a hub-and-spokes system. Most levels have some type of hub with the objectives branching off from it. That way we can still have some parts that are kind of linear and familiar to the player, while still letting them have the freedom of decision.

MK: Is there anything else you would like to share with players?

RD: Experiment with landing choices. You can get a completely different experience depending on your landing choice as well as which objectives you go after first. An example is the town hall in Operation Husky. Trying to fight your way in from the town square is really hard and you might keep dying. Landing on the roof is a completely different experience. Get creative and try to think outside of the linear trough that you are used to.

Also, we set out to change the FPS genre, and that's what I think we've done. We are really satisfied with the results. We are going to be here for a while. We've got a Triple-A team and we're going to keep the franchise going.

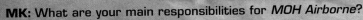

MICHAEL LICHT—MISSION LEAD

MK: What are your main responsibilities for *MOH Airborne*?

ML: Early prototyping for the levels. Level design had to be worked out for the player to land anywhere. And then the AI to work with it. Later on, mission design, early layout docs, then oversee other levels. I helped out on Husky and was the Lead on Avalanche and Market Garden

MK: Since *MOH Airborne* is very open in its gameplay rather than scripted, what challenges did you face in designing these missions?

ML: Getting the interesting experiences you get from a linear game in a game where you can drop anywhere. How do we craft the environment? How do we focus the player toward the objectives? And performance—how can we get this all in and still have it work?

Everyone expects *MOH* to be a very crafted experience with the cinematics and such. The hard part for us is, how do we know where the player is going to be so we can set the cameras up? What is interesting is that the more we let go of trying to control where the player was going to be, and the more we started thinking he could be anywhere in this area, we need to make sure no matter where he lands he gets a good view, then it really wasn't that hard. The more we tried to focus the player, the more things were breaking. By leaving it more open, with less walls, then it seemed to work better.

MK: What is the process you go through when designing a

mission?

ML: We start with the most simple diagram: What is sort of the pattern you want it to go in? Then we have graphic artists and artists start pulling up references. We know where it is going to be, what timeframe, what the situation is going to be, so let's get some pictures and put it all on the whiteboard. We get the dry erasers out, figure out what the objectives will be and, board after board after board, we get a rough diagram and, if you squint your eyes, you can kind of see the map. That is the point where we start working on a 2-D. I don't let them start a 3-D until we have a reasonably agreed upon map and design document that describes all the objectives, all the special events, etc. As a result, there was little deviation from the beginning 3-D work to the final because it had all been planned out before. I have a Master's in architecture and that was the way I was trained. You do all the preliminary work, plan it all out, before you even go near a shovel.

MK: Is there something in the game of which you are particularly proud?

ML: I wanted to bring the game back to the player. We want players to go to their friends and say, "You won't believe what I did in *Medal of Honor Airborne*." You can't do that in linear games because he'll say "Yeah, I did the same thing." We want them to have a sense of accomplishment. Take your time, play the maps, upgrade your weapons, explore every crevice, have fun.

TIMOTHY FORD—LEAD AI DESIGNER, SOFTWARE ENGINEER

MK: How did the new AI technology come about?

TF: When we started working on *Airborne*, we did not know what the drop would bring to the game. We then realized that you give control to the player, and when you do that and the player can land anywhere, not only do you have to have an environment that is big enough and rich enough for choices of where to land, you also have to have a technology that can handle it. The player is not going to be coming down a pipe to each engagement. They can come from the front, from the rooftops, from the rear, from some other flank. Our existing technology would not work for this. We prototyped with engines from *MOH Pacific Assault* and other *MOH* games, but they wouldn't work. The encounters could only played from one particular direction or the engagement would break. So we developed the Affordance Engine.

MK: What is the Affordance Engine in a nutshell?

TF: A solution where the AI can use the environment to their advantage against the player—a player that can attack from any direction either with his allies or by himself.

MK: Does the allied AI use it as well?

TF: Yes, they do. In fact, they actually try to teach the player early on to look for affordances or terrain that will give him an advantage over the enemy. They do this by modeling the behavior. They will always take cover. If there is a machine gun, they will man it. They get the player thinking, "How can I use that?"

MK: Is the engine modeled after something?

TF: Yes, we based it on the tactics of the German army, scaled down to a smaller scale. In war, soldiers usually were not so close to the enemy. For the game, we wanted to make it more intimate. You are in closer proximity to the enemy than you would be in real life.

MK: How does the enemy detect you?

TF: You could theoretically play the game stealthily, but it is very difficult since the enemy turn their heads a lot. They will hear you reload, switch weapons, walking too fast, etc. Threat is an even bigger drive than detection.

MK: How do you get the enemy AI to respond? What are their priorities?

TF: They have an order of threats to which they respond:

1. The enemy shot at me.
2. The enemy killed someone next to me.
3. The enemy blew my cover, so the cover is no longer protecting me.
4. I can see the enemy.
5. The enemy is near me.

The higher-level enemies will move around and try to flank you, especially if you are behind cover and not firing at them.

MK: How does the friendly AI (U.S. paratroopers) react and respond to the player's actions?

TF: They will use similar tactics to the enemy as well as other things. When you start to lose health, they will start to help you more rather than just moving to the objective. If you kill enemies and clear an area, they will move up and claim it. If you are near them when they are about to move up, they will say something like "Cover me" to coax the player to move up. If they see a mounted gun position or a grenade on the ground, they will point it out. They will provide suppressing fire for you and for each other. If you provide suppressing fire when the allies are moving up, they are a lot more likely to survive getting to new cover.

MK: Is there something you want players to know about the game, that they would not realize for themselves?

TF: *MOHA* offers the player an experience unique to the player's playing style, to the player's obsession. The only way the player will notice that is to play the same level twice in different ways. The weapon selection also adds variety. You are going to play a mission differently with a sniper rifle than you would with a shotgun. The experience you are having with this game is your own. No one playing the same mission is going to have the exact same experience that you had.

TOM HESS—MULTIPLAYER GAMEPLAY PRODUCER

MK: What previous projects have you worked on?

TH: *MOH Breakthrough* and *MOH Pacific Assault*

MK: What are your main responsibilities for *MOH Airborne*? Which do you consider the most challenging, and why?

TH: To get the multiplayer done and fun. The biggest challenge was how to leverage the single-player game to make multiplayer more fun.

MK: What makes the multiplayer game in *MOH Airborne* different from other games?

TH: The airdrop sets it apart from everything else. Unlike in single-player, you can jump anywhere. The maps are smaller and everything is in the drop zone. You spawn in the air and instantly the whole world is below you. The enemies are running around like little ants and you can land behind them to take them out or land somewhere safe, like through a hole in the roof. Every time you spawn, you can make decisions based on looking at the world below you. Also, the entire map is playable.

MK: How did you go about making the maps for multiplayer?

TH: We used three maps from *MOH Allied Assault* and had to next-gen them, add roofs since they didn't have originally, and make it so you can land anywhere. We also had to make ways for the Axis to get up on top of the buildings. There are also three maps from the single-player missions. Since those were huge, we played around in them and found areas that were interesting, then sectioned them off to create a smaller play area.

MK: Do you have a goal for the way the multiplayer games are played?

TH: We want players to strategize and play together—especially in the Objective Airborne games. For the games with airdrops, we also want the Allies to be looking down to plan where they should land and the Axis players to be looking up to try to either shoot the enemy in the air or position themselves for when they land.

MK: What strategy or tactic do you use during multiplayer games?

TH: Start with the automatic weapons since they are easier to use. Fire them in short bursts.

SPECIAL THANKS
Prima would like to thank Bryce Yang and the team.

MEDAL OF HONOR™ AIRBORNE
PUBLISHED BY ELECTRONIC ARTS
A PRODUCTION OF ELECTRONIC ARTS LOS ANGELES

Executive Producer
Patrick Gilmore

Senior Development Director
Jeff Charvat

Technical Director
Mark Dochtermann

Creative Director
Jon Paquette

Audio Director
Paul Lackey

Art Director
Justin Thomas

Production Designer
Ken Harsha

Computer Graphics Director
James H. Dargie

Producers
Christopher A. Busse
Tom Hess
Matt Marsala
Neville Spiteri
TJ Stamm

Development Directors
Kevin Hendrickson
Audrea Topps-Harjo
Patrick Hurd
Michael Saladino
Meg Sheehan

Lead Designer
Rex Dickson

Lead Engineer
Simon Myszko

AI Lead
Timothy Ford

Lead Character Artist
Eoin Colgan

Lead Environment Artist
Waylon Brinck

Lead Lighter
Rachel Mina

Lead Visual Effects Artist
David Oliver

Lead Animator
Eric Smith

Lead Concept Artist
Toby Wilson

Community Manager
Justin "BlackHat" Korthof

Project Coordinator
Jada Brazil

EALA General Manager
Neil Young

DESIGN TEAM
Designers
Joe DiDonato
S. Ryan Heaton
Robert Bruce Heck
James Kono
Chad LaClair
Josh Leyshock
Michael Licht
Kevin Mack
Stephen Riesenberger
Edwin Rodriguez
Paul Valdivia
Tamar Zeithlian

Design Interns
Chris DeLeon
Kwasi Mensah
Herb Yang

ENGINEERING TEAM
Systems Engineers
Jimmy Alamparambil
Pedro Arroyo
Edward Beranek
Scott Carter
Steve Chow
Randy Dillon
Jerome Lanquetot
Tom McDevitt
Ben Vance

Gameplay Engineers
Omar Aziz
Jim DiNunzio
Mona Fawzy
Frantz Joseph
Michael Kron
Donald Lawton
Darryll Rohr
Matthew Tonks
Andrew Wang
Mia Watanabe

Multiplayer Engineers
Jeff Dubrule
Chris Jacobson
Robert Memmott
Lee Saito
Jake Warmerdam

Central Audio Technology
David Cham
Eduardo Trama

Configuration Management
Dave Fox
Blair Hamilton
Jason Micklewright

Interns
Ankur Ahlawat
Torin Kampa
Kinshuk Mishra
Giray Ozil
Rohith Ravindranath
Benjamin Weber

ART TEAM
Animators
Umberto Bossi
Kole Lasekan
Gilbert Ngo
Garrett Shikuma
Robert Weaver

Concept Artists
Daniel Cheng
Chris Miller
Rich Olson

Character Artists
Beau Anderson
Huy Dinh
Glenda Novotny

Environment Artists
Jay Ardiosa
Joon Choi
Anupam Das
Takehiro Hattori
Sean Higgins
Thao Le
Anup Lobo
Chris McLeod
Heather Poon
Lance Powell
Phelicia Ramlogan
Josh Robinson
Art Wong

Lighters
Michael Comly
David Kintner
George Rushing

Associate CG Supervisor
Shinichiro Hara

Visual Effects Artist
Michael Dudley

Technical Artist
Eben Cook

Character Riggers
Jeremy Carson
Billy Shih

UI Artist
Michael Tamura

Asset Integration
Michael Aarsvold
Armando Castillo
Brian Clarke
Chris Hands

Character Model
Jed Boegar Bernard

AUDIO TEAM
Audio Designers
Aaron Brown
Jade Kao
Tyler Parsons
Leilani Ramirez
Jeff Wilson

Dialogue and Digital Asset Management
Bobby Moldavon

Intern
Dan Lehrich

Voice Over Talent
Brian Bloom
Alberto Brosio
Danny Cooksey
Nino Delprete
Eddie Frierson
Luciano Giancarlo
Peter Giles
Johnny Hawkes
Andrew Heffernan
Brian Herskowitz
Matt Lindquist
Yuri Lowenthal
Scott Menville
Jonathan Nichols
Chris Ogden
Luciano Palmeri
Skip Stellrecht
Pepper Sweeney
Emmanuel Todorov
Ariana Weil
Dave Wittenberg
Kai Wulff
Victor Yerrid

VIDEO TEAM
Video Director
Drew Stauffer

EPOXY Group
Senior Development Director
David Schwartz

Development Manager
Kate Bigel

Project Managers
Vicky Kwan
Marissa Carus
Edu Black

Vendor Coordinator
Alexis Beamon

Director of Pipeline/Process
Richard Brous

GLOBAL ONLINE STUDIO
Development Director
Lars Smith

Producers
Tom DuBois
Shawn Stafford

Engineers
Ashley Bennett
Ryan Butterfoss
Joey Carruthers

TECHNICAL ADVISORS
Technical Advisor
Martin K. A. Morgan

Research/Historical Advisors
11th Kompanie
1SG Lewis H. Mikulecky
Gale R. Ammerman
The Collings Foundation
D Company, 505th Parachute
Infantry
Frazer Brothers
George H. Leidenheimer
Living History Corp at the
National D-Day Museum
The National D-Day Museum
Don Rubin
Suzanne Nicole Sundahl
SSgt. Quay L. K. Terry USMC

ADDITIONAL PRODUCT SUPPORT
Additional Producers
Brady Bell
Nina Dobner
Dan Elggren
Jon Galvan
Craig Jepson
Dylan Kohler
Darion Lowenstein
Anthony Miller
Christopher Plummer
Matt Sentell

Additional DDs
Thor Alexander
Ray Cobo
Rob Elser
Mario Grimani
David Kury
Larry Paolicelli
Greg Salter
John Salwitz
Anthony Schmill
David Seeholzer

Additional Production
Lisa Beard

Additional Design
Jason Alejandre
Christian Chang
Nathan Cox
Adam Crist
Paul Cross
Casey Kuczik
Ed Moore
Benson Russell

Additional Engineering
Adriano Antonio
John Ballantyne
Richard Benson
Stuart Capewell
Justin Chang
Lan-Fang Chang
Shu Cheah
Ben Deane
Jason Gregory
Tolga Kart
Paul Keet
Jeffrey Leggett
Jason Lenny
Daniel Levesque
Mike Machowski
Dave Mercier
Zak Middleton
Vikram Nerurkar
Eric Phister
Tim Probst
Richard Robaina
Luis Sempe
Blazej Stompel
Wei Shoong Teh

Additional Art
Billy Brooks
Jennifer Cha
Ili Chiang
Shaun Comly
John Decker
Bruce Ferriz
Jose Flores
Jeff Gregory
Paul Jury
Oliver Leeman
Tony Montana
Jason Monroe
Chris Oakley
Marvin Rojas
Emile Smith
Robert Stahl
Peter Tieryas

Tonya Tornberg
Dan Whiting

Additional Audio
Gregory Allen
Aaron Berkson
Lexa Burton
Jeremy Hall
Erik Kraber
Scott Lawlor
Mario Lavin
Andy Martin
Charles Maynes

EXTERNAL DEVELOPMENT TEAMS

Active8
Executive Manager
David Zhu

Development Director
Yao Bin

Lead Artist
Jin Xi Zeng

Lead Level Artist
Li Peng Xiang

Level Artists
Li Ming, You Quan, Zhu Jia Min

Lead Model Artist
Ni Chuan Long

Model Artists
Li Wei, Zhu Lei
Wang Wei
Qiao Yu Qin
Cao Lei
Huang Hai
Sun Hui
Ma Yan Rong
Yu Sen
Yang Ying

Engineer
Zhang Shi Yang

Demiurge Studios
Lead Producer
Albert Reed

Lead Engineers
Kurt Reiner

Lead Environment Artists
Tom Lin

Designers
Dan Chretien
Jason D. Lentz

Systems Engineers
Michael Breen
Roger Hanna
Andy Hendrickson
Rob Jagnow
Christopher Linder
Bill McFadden
Andrew Moise
Alex Rice

Environment Artists
Andrew Cormier
Dave Flamburis
Katie Stampf

Technical Artist
Magnolia Caswell-Mackey

Quality Assurance Lead
Evan Nikolich

Quality Assurance Testers
Maria O'Brien
Jimmy Storey
Mike Ace White

Business Management
Bill Reed

Papaya Studio
Lead Engineer
Laurent Horisberger

Engineering Team
Rosen Baklov
Matt Fawcett
Niall Ryan

Additional Production
Lin Shen

Ritual Entertainment, Inc.
Systems Engineers
Aaron Cole
Squirrel Eiserloh
Eric Fowler
Ken Harward
Scott Inglis
Roger Kort
Chris Stark
Chris Willis-Ford

System Administrators
Mason Lucas

Concept Artists
Robert Atkins

Environmental Artists
Gary Buchanan
Chris Curra
Aaron Hausmann
Bobby Hutson
Kristian Kane
Hector Marquez
Ethan McCaughey
James O'Donnell
Nick Pappas
Kevin Penrod
Mike Penrod
Ivan Villavicencio

Designers
John Boyd
Ian Childs
Jesse Flanagan
Russell Meakim
Todd Rose
John Schuch

Project Coordinators
Drew Jensen
Tom Mustaine

QUALITY ASSURANCE

QA Project Lead
Salvador Delgado

QA Lead Tester
Dave Baer
Sean Manzano

QA Engineers
Sergio Flores
Kumar Iyer
Steven Hoey

QA Senior Testers
Nicholas Clifford
Jeremy Feasel
Graeham Ford
Jared Greene
Paul John Jochico
Willian Penn III
Louie Soriano
Chase Swanson
Vanessa Zuloaga

QA Testers
Sarah Aanerud
Jorge Aguayo
Nickolas Anderson
Ron Avila
Humberto Braga
Zephirin Broussard
Steven Callahan
Steve Cantu
Simon Castillo
Innokenty Chugai
Hugo Conchucos
Nicholas Cruzado
Kevin Dandridge
Jeff Dipietro
Keith Evans
Gil Fischel
Dan Friedman
Dean Gagliano
Todd Gershon
Grant Glazer
Anthony Gordon
Manuel Grimaldo
Marvin Jacksoin
Jason Jacoby
Ryan James
Arielle Jayme
Josh Johnson
Robby Kushner
Joseph Lagana
Jonathan Landis
Braxton Lee
David Levin
Albert Lien
Samuel Mackey
Jeff Magers
Charles Mallison
Matthew Manning
Barton Marks
Brendt McKnight
Larry McZeal
Nathan Mobley
Cesar Muralles
Michael Norris
Zachary Owens

Brian Paoloni
David Pelayo
Joseph Perez
Catalin Petrescu
Joshua Pletzke
Sunny Poon
Manuel Reynolds
Joshua Rotunda
AJ Smith
Anthony Smith
Stephen Stalker
Jeffrey Tessar
Michael Thomas
Christian Velasquez
Christopher Velez
Tajlammar Void
Joey Wellman
Bryan Wilbur

EALA LEADERSHIP

Chief Operating Officer
Darrell Rodriguez

Chief Technology Officer
Marcel Samek

Chief Financial Officer
Christina Sawyer

Director, Human Resources
Susan Otto

LOCALIZATION

Director, Studio Operations / Localization
Thilo Huebner

Localization Manager
Joel Börjel

European Localization Production
Isabel Guijarro Bonald
Sergio Vargas

European Localization Coordination
Thomas Baerdorff
Enrico Lupo Balducci
Iván Barreras
Chantal Cervoni
Frederic Champ
Álvaro Corral
Lucas Dupleix
Alessio De Fazio
Martin Eriksson
Kasia Gryglewska-Cebrat
Fabio Maccari
Nadine Monschau
Alfonsina Mossello
Jakub Nowicki
Paweł Paszkowski
Pavel Rutski
David Suarez
Dominika Szot
Iñaki Valladares

European Localization Programming
Mario Bergantiños
Iñigo Bermejo

Eduardo Cocero Torres
Felipe González López
Danilo José Guerrero Rodríguez
Alberto Marín Ibañez
Patrick C. Payne
César Puerta
Miguel Angel Rodríguez González
Antonio Yago

European Localization Team
Anatole
Raul Barahona
Andres Berral
Robert Böck
Stefania Caravello
Fausto Ceccarelli
Israel Delgado
Karolis Dzevecka
Estudios EXA
Dorothee Garth
toneworx GmbH
Javier Gonzalez Diez
Norbert Horvath
Alexander Kornberg
Maciej Kos
Daniel Kroner
Eugeny Kuchigin
Liliana Morosini
Marco Nicolino
Roman Rodriguez
Luis M. Ruano
Jose Ramon Santamarina
Javier Somoza
Jan Stanicek
Maciej Sytar
Gergő Szendy
Hervé Throuilh
Le Trait d'Union

Asian Localization Production
Jason Chen
Nice Lee
Ryan Reiji
Jazz Wang

Asian Localization Coordination
Diane Ng

Asian Localization Programming
Abdool Gafoor
Kiong Hieng Ong
Lei Tan
Frank Wang

Asian Localization Team
Jianwei Chin
Mitsuo Iijima
Sky Lin
Robin Lian
Yuan Wei Adrian Lim
Seiichi Nakamura
Chin Ang Ng
Rizal Raub
Atsuko Saso
Eileen Su
Takeshi Sugiura
Miki Suzuki
Takaaki Suzuki
Derek Tan
Lei Tan

Tuck Yee Tham
Jijin Yang
Bonam Yu

MOTION CAPTURE

Motion Capture Facility
EA World Wide Motion Capture Studio

Motion Capture Lead
Vince Ng
John Mayhew

Additional Motion Capture
Sara Cameron
Eldon Derksen
Atlin Fraser
Ryan Hietanen
Blair Leckie
Cory Permack
Kristy Sorgard
Marie Tai

Motion Capture Talent
Jeffrey Fisher
Damien King
Paul Lazenby
Brett Queen
Jason Wingham
Donovan Stinson

MUSIC TEAM

Executive Music Producer
Steve Schnur

Music By
Michael Giacchino

Orchestrators
Tim Simonec
Chris Tilton
Jennifer Hammond
Marshall Bowen
Chad Seiter
Mark Gasbarro
Larry Kenton
Peter Boyer
Dominik Hauser
Brad Dechter

Music Copyist
Gregg Nestor

Conducted by
Tim Simonec
Richard Rintoul

Contracted by
Reggie Wilson
Connie Boylan

Recorded and Mixed by
Dan Wallin

Recordist
Greg Dennen
Paul Wertheimer

Score Assistant
Andrea Datzman

Music Editor
Alex Levy

Assistant to Music Editor
Paul Apelegren

Recorded at the Eastwood Scoring Stage and Paramount Stage "M"

EALA MASTERING LAB
Louis Burgueno
John Freeman
James Geiger

MARKETING AND PUBLIC RELATIONS

Marketing VP
Clive Downie

Marketing Director
Craig Owens

Product Manager
Jim Ferris

Public Relations Manager
Brooke Cahalane

Marketing Assistant
Bryce Yang

Marketing Assistant/Assistant Video Editor
Abby Zirkle

Marketing Video Editor
Christopher Harris

European Marketing Team
Rafael Martinez
Peter O'Reilly

Asia Pacific Team
Liam McCallum
Karen Polson
Sergio A. Salvador
Nana Takahashi

Documentation
Sharon Ortiz

Documentation Layout
John Burns
Nathan Carrico

Additional Marketing and PR:
Simon Bull
Sara Marshall
Mike Maser
Jon Rissik
Abby Topolsky

This game is not endorsed by, approved by, or associated with the U.S. Department of Defense.

SPECIAL THANKS

To everyone at EALA for their support, especially Louis Castle, Doug Church, Mike Verdu, and all the other product teams at EALA, and Jonathan Lutz, Peter Navin, Arcadia Kim, Alex Plachowski, Joe Aguilar, David Alvarez, Steve Arnold, Vanessa Auerswald, Staci Goddard, Wayne Hall, Charles Hamilton, Jimmie Harlow, Jason Harrell, Tu Holmes, Isaac Lee, William Lee, Michael Levitt, Mick Love, Daniel Pickett, Charles Polanski, Keith Price, Ray Robinson, Tim Sabourin, Scott Sinnott, Chris Taylor. And to everyone at Electronic Arts for their support: John Riccitiello, Bing Gordon, Warren Jenson, Paul Lee, Frank Gibeau, Gerhard Florin, John Schappert, Gabrielle Toledano, Glenn Entis, Joel Linzner, Patrick O'Brien, Marci Galea, Sue Garfield, Jake Schatz, Customer Quality Control, European Certification Group, WW Audit crew, Scott Taylor, Tom Boyd, and Bharat Vasan, and everyone else at Electronic Arts.

Development Team
The team would like to thank their family and friends. Without their support, this game would not have been possible: Allana; Michael K. Anderson; Xylia Arroyo; Campbell Askew; The Beranek Family; Valerie R. Lewis and Gregory B. Brazil; Brooks, Judy, and Randy Brown; Magnolia Busse; Jeremy Cain; Crocko and El Capitan; The Cham Family; Diane, Jeffrey and Danny Charvat; Evan Chen; Jenny and Isabella Chow; Lisa Christey; The Colgan Clan; Sunshine Cook; Tim Coolidge; Robin and Sophia Dargie; Narayan and Shapna Das and the Das family; Ryan Davidson; Rebecca and Henry Deane; Deborah; Mike DiDonato; Marianna, Random and Rhyme Dochtermann; Stephanie Dudley; Kristin Fitzsimmons; Jen Fox; Meg Marie Ford; Sarah Garbett; Rena Hattori; Christy Hendrickson and the Hendrickson Family; Cristina Garza; Bruce and Maria Heck; Felicity and Zoie Hendricks; Wako Huang; Patricia Jacobson; Sandhya and Jasmine; El Jorge; Dan King; Amy Kono; Anne Sawell, Cole and Bryn Lackey; Emilie Lanquetot; Yemisi and Funmilayo Lasekan; Andrew, Rebecca, Emilio, Michela and Shawn Lawlor; Lydia Lee; Sunny Lee; Winnie and Aaron (the 1st airborne baby) Licht; Mechelle Lois and Toshi Carson-Lois; Lorrie; Helena, Charlie, Anna and Pocky Marsala; Danielle, Samantha and Maxwell; Minou and crossie; Barbara, Sherman, Ida, and Casey Moldavon; Jennie Morse; Ms. Panda; Mary and Isabelle Paquette; William Perkins; The Poon family; Ian "The Professional" Porter; Koa Ramirez; Shawna Rohr; Sarah, Delia; Lila, and Rome; Evelyn Schiff; Anthony Scott; The Sheehan Family; Amber Dempsey Shikuma; Trevor Somers; The Spiteri Family; Sara and Phoebe Stein; Setsu, Marinah, and Yasmine Tamura; Yolanda Tang; Sandra Thomas; Aja Reign Topps-Harjo; Avery Goldstein and Marlon Trama; Yaleny Valdes; Kelly Valdivia, and the Valdivia family; The Valentin Family; Yumiko Wilson; Anita Yip.

The Airborne team would also like to thank members of the 82nd Airborne, currently active or retired from service. And to all the United States armed forces around the world, to Mike "Sarge" Embley, to Victoria Leslie and others who work for the Congressional Medal of Honor Society, to the National World War II Museum, the Imperial War Museum, the Airborne Museum Hartenstein, and to combat re-enactors, historic warbird owners, pilots, and restorers, you have been an inspiration to us in the making of this game.

Finally, the team would like to give their special thanks to the passionately devoted *Medal of Honor* community. You guys rock!

BIBLIOGRAPHY

Blumenson, Martin. *US Army in World War II: Salerno to Cassino*. Washington, D.C.: Center of Military History, 1993.

Garland, Albert N., Lt. Col., and Howard McGraw Smyth. *US Army in World War II: Sicily and the Surrender of Italy*. Washington, D.C.: Center of Military History, 1993.

Harrison, Gordon A. *US Army in World War II: Cross-Channel Attack*. Washington, D.C.: Center of Military History, 1993.

MacDonald, Charles B. *US Army in World War II: The Last Offensive*. Washington, D.C.: Center of Military History, 1993.

———. *US Army in World War II: The Siegfried Line Campaign*. Washington, D.C.: Center of Military History, 1993.

Megellas, James. *All the Way to Berlin*. New York: Random House, 2003.

Perret, Geoffrey. *There's a War to be Won: The United States Army in World War II*. New York, Ballantine Books, 1991.

Rottman, Gordon L. *US Airborne Units in the Mediterranean Theater 1942–44*. New York: Osprey Publishing, 2006.

———. *World War II Airborne Warfare Tactics*. New York: Osprey Publishing, 2006.

Smith, Carl. *US Paratrooper 1941–1945*. New York: Osprey Publishing, 2000.

Zaloga, Steven J. *US Airborne Units in the ETO 1944–45*. New York: Osprey Publishing, 2007.

———. *Utah Beach and the US Airborne Landings*. New York: Osprey Publishing, 2004.

MEDAL OF HONOR
AIRBORNE